I0816306

A HOUSE TO *call home*

CHRISTIE PURIFOY

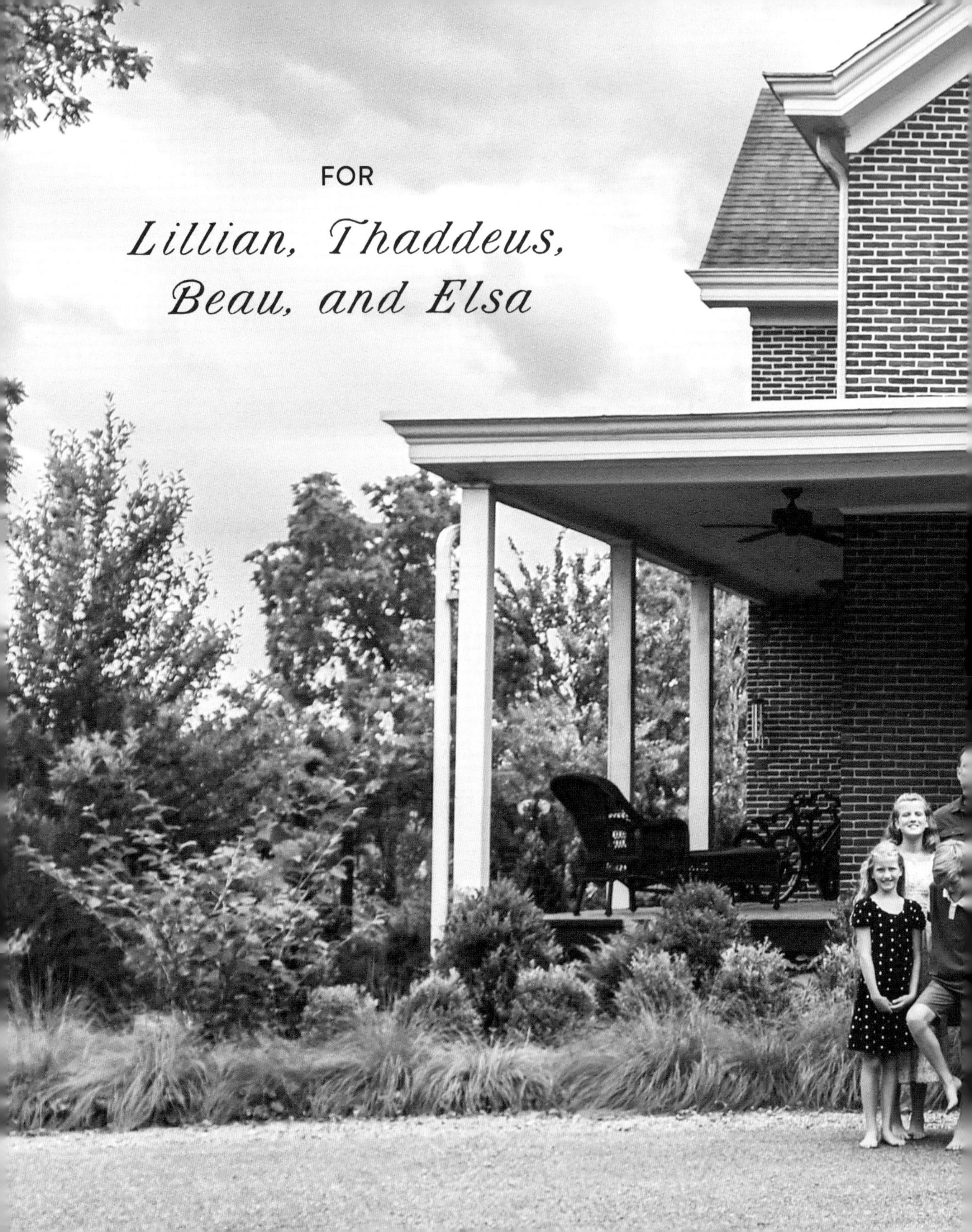

FOR

Lillian, Thaddeus, Beau, and Elsa

CONTENTS

You Are Welcome in This Place

Those were the words I seemed to hear whispered between two rows of sentinel maple trees when Jonathan and I first drove down the long driveway toward the comforting redbrick face of the house called Maplehurst. Of course, I did not speak the language of trees then, and I am only a novice now, but I was aware from the beginning that here was a house we could call home. Despite the summer heat wave and the heaviness of my unborn daughter, the dim, un-air-conditioned rooms beckoned like a spacious place. As I climbed one flight of stairs and another and another, as I stepped in and out of small attic bedrooms, I knew that if there was a life too large for this house, it would be a life I did not want. Here was a house that could hold all of our dreams and desires, our love and our living. Even our grief would be welcome here.

We were not grieving then; we were simply desperate. Our fourth baby was about to be born, but we did not want our life with her to begin in Florida, a place that sometimes felt like a wilderness and sometimes felt like an oasis of rest but never felt like home. Here, then, was where our life as a family of six would begin and where it would grow. Here in this quiet green corner of Pennsylvania, in the redbrick house that Quaker farmers built, we would make a place together for ourselves and for others. Florida had given too much of too few things: too much sunshine, too much heat, and row after row of unchangeable longleaf pine trees. I would have loved it for a vacation, but I did not know how to love it as a home. In Pennsylvania, I found a place of constant, subtle alteration. Here, the seasons are always shifting, the clouds coming and going, the trees budding,

greening, coloring, falling. And at the center of it all is the abiding stillness of the house.

Many years after our move to Maplehurst, my friend Amy—a friend I had known in Texas as a child and found again as a near neighbor in Pennsylvania—passed on to me something she had once heard a teacher say: seen from a certain angle, the Bible has only three chapters. The first is "Home." The second is "Lost." The third is "Home Again." This is a universal story, and it has been for me a very personal story. A search for home first led us to a farmhouse at the top of a gentle hill, but this place has become the foundation for a life of continual homecoming and

FINE TEAS
HARNEY & SONS
MASTER TEA BLENDERS
EST. 1983
LAPSANG
SOUCHONG
CHINESE BLACK TEA
25-30 CUPS
HANDPACKED IN MILLERTON, NY
NET WT. 3 OZ./85G

perpetual arrival, as if home is a house always able to welcome us into deeper versions of itself.

A faithful life is a journeying life. It is, as an itinerant rabbi with no place to lay his own head once said, a *Way*, and as long as we are traveling, it is possible to become a little lost. You can stay in one place and still days will come when you do not know where you are. On those days when I feel lost again, the very same house that I have tended and repaired and tried to make beautiful has wrapped its arms around me. The same house I have given as comfort to others has offered its comfort to me. And when I use the word *comfort*, I do not mean anything sentimental or self-indulgent. I am excavating the ancient origins of this word: *fort* means "strength." Centuries before this word spoke to us of material ease, before we ever imagined comfort foods or getting out of our comfort zone, the earliest English-language Bibles used the name *Comforter* for God's Spirit in our midst. To give and receive comfort is to give and receive the deepest kind of strength, the kind necessary if we are to live our lives well. And a life well lived is a powerful force in a world desperate for meaning, direction, and hope. I try not to retreat into my home to hide—either from the world or from myself. I retreat into my home to rest, to heal, and to be replenished for another day of whole-hearted living. I like to think others have also found this kind of retreat here at Maplehurst. We are not all called to be placemakers, but we are all in need of the comfort good places can give.

I am not the same woman who came home to this house twelve years ago, but then this place is not the same either. The making of a place can be the making of a person. Common sense may tell us that gardens grow but places do not, that maple trees change according to the seasons but a house called Maplehurst must stay essentially the same. A house cannot gain a bedroom because a daughter is born or shrink a dining room because two children have left for college. Yet change is growth and growth is life, and beloved places are filled with life. Making a place is not like making a picture that does not shift or change. It is more like making a garden that grows as we care for it.

Making a place is not like making a picture that does not shift or change. It is more like making a garden that grows as we care for it.

Twelve years in this Pennsylvania farmhouse—years lived between the birth of a daughter, the arrival of a mother-in-law, and the departure of two older children—have shown me a mysterious truth: places *can* change, though it is less like a child's wild growth and more like a tree's accumulation of one more ring.

When we first came to this Victorian farmhouse with three small children and one more on the way, I had an insistent question: does making a place matter? Is it worth the sacrifice of time and energy and resources? I know now that it does matter, that it matters very much, but I also know that life brings seasons of making, of unmaking, and of making anew. Places are not static. They are more like people, more like trees, and they have a life of their own that must be tended so that they in turn can take care of us. This is a book about the life of one particular old house, the house I know best, the one that has been the making of me. Its life began before I ever came here, and its life will continue long after I am gone. The life of this house is utterly unique, and yet I am more and more convinced that all well-loved places can be havens for rest and welcome, healing and comfort. With care and creativity, all houses can be called home.

PARADISE AND PLENTY

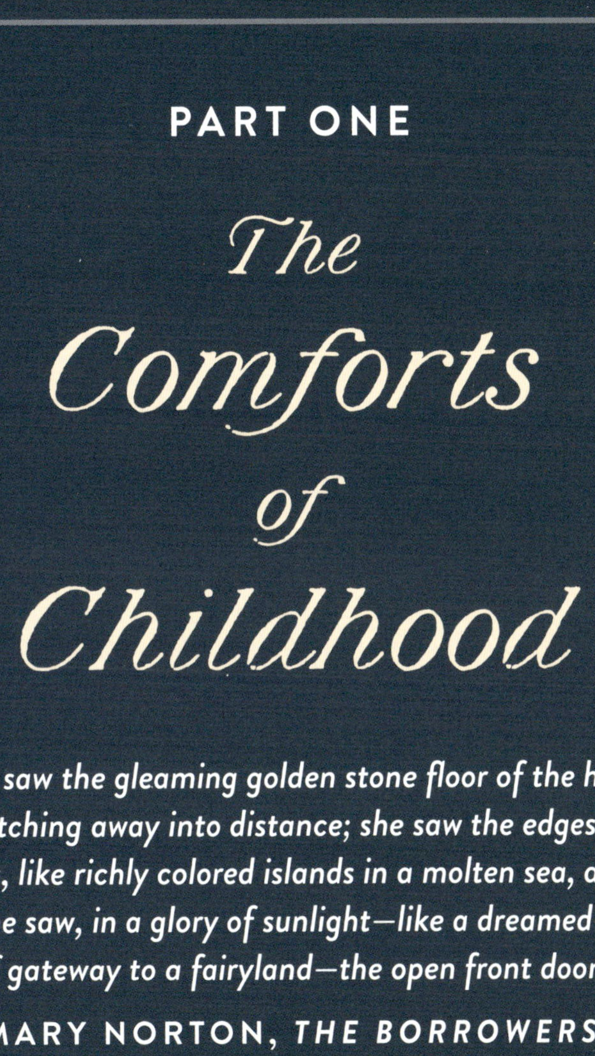

PART ONE

The Comforts of Childhood

She saw the gleaming golden stone floor of the hall stretching away into distance; she saw the edges of rugs, like richly colored islands in a molten sea, and she saw, in a glory of sunlight—like a dreamed-of gateway to a fairyland—the open front door.

MARY NORTON, *THE BORROWERS*

(Doll) House Repairs

When I was four, I moved with my parents and two younger sisters to a small brick house on Jersey Street in a Texas college town. In my mind, it seems we had hardly unpacked our boxes before my parents were wallpapering the far end of the front room that would serve as our dining nook. The care they lavished on this corner spot where two walls hugged our heavy, dark dining suite had a quality of reverence. Of course, I would not then have used that word. I only knew that in a period of immense transition (*which* box held my enormous mustard-yellow teddy bear?), this papering of the walls, this careful measuring of mitered corners for a wooden chair rail that would frame the new paper like art, mattered in ways I accepted but could not yet understand.

My father was a university campus minister. When I picture him as he was then, he holds a soft leather Bible and he is leading a group in prayer, or he is gardening, or he is repairing or redecorating our house. I cannot say these tasks held equal value to him, but as his firstborn observer, I envisioned them as lying on a single plane of importance. We were followers of the Jesus way in the Baptist tradition, which meant we offered hospitality, which meant we took care with our home, which meant wallpaper was sacred, though *sacred* was not a word we used in our family.

My own first foray into home repairs came around the age of ten when, after much begging from his three daughters, my father built for us a plywood dollhouse. My sisters and I had begun collecting miniatures after discovering a dollhouse shop while away from our Texas home on a Colorado vacation. My first miniature was a tiny bakery cake,

dolloped with tiny plaster frosting, and looking real enough to eat, though one swallow would have taken care of it. The tiny cake was followed by a tiny ice-cream-parlor seating set. The two chairs had curvy wire backs and the table legs were swoops of golden wire. These were soon followed by a ceramic kitten lapping up a ceramic puddle of milk, a set of three old-fashioned flour bags, and half a dozen paper books about the size of my father's thumbnail. Obviously, these precious possessions required a home of their own.

That Christmas I was entrusted with my mother's glue gun in order to attach rows of tiny wooden shingles to the plywood roof of the gift I now shared with my sisters. I can remember standing on a chair in my blue corduroy jumper and daubing each shingle with glue before adding it to an overlapping row. Gossamer strands of hot glue settled on the roof like cobwebs.

My best friend, Molly, shared my love for tiny replicas. Her parents were not "in ministry," so the exquisite dollhouse she received that Christmas came ready-made from the fanciest dollhouse shop in the greater Houston metro area. Every item was perfectly to scale, which meant that when I peered into the rooms, I felt suddenly aware of myself as a giant before slipping seamlessly into the doll family's point of view. I especially envied my friend the soft felt fuzz of her wall-to-wall carpeting. My own dollhouse was carpeted with remnants from my father's redecorating, which meant that the pile was so deep my doll family's feet would entirely disappear into it.

Molly and I grew apart in middle school. We briefly reconnected after high school graduation, but our reunion was short-lived. While we were both still teenagers, my friend was killed in an accident involving cars and alcohol and a courtroom trial of which the only memory I can call to mind involves me seated between my mother and Molly's mother and noticing the familiar face of our fifth-grade teacher amongst the jury. *Was this allowed? Our former teacher on the jury, the one who had read* Where the Red Fern Grows *to both of us?* Who knew what was right in this strange, unforeseen world of young adulthood. Immediately after my friend had died and long before the trial, my mother and I went to her home to, in my mother's words, "pay our respects," and I sat quietly with a group of old school friends and our mothers in the dining room where the only sign of my friend's life was her dollhouse sitting on the floor in a corner of the room. I did not ask to see it, but everything in me wanted to move to the floor, open the swinging front panel of the house I knew so well, and grow small again.

Not long after, I married my high school sweetheart, graduated from college, and moved away from Texas, but I would return every year or so to see family. Sometimes I would run into my friend's mother at the shopping mall in my small hometown, and I felt guilty with each new update I gave, acutely aware that my friend had not lived long enough to marry or move away, to buy her first house or become a mother. On one of those visits, I despaired at the sight of my old dollhouse sitting, dilapidated, in my parents' garage. After I grew up, it had been played with by so many visiting children—my parents' ministry hospitality was legendary—that it hurt to look too closely at the run-down house with its broken shingles. I collected a few of my favorite bits and pieces and brought them home to my own firstborn daughter.

Eventually my little girl added the bakery cake and the kitten lapping milk to a dollhouse her grandfather, my husband's father, built for her from a dollhouse kit. Her house was a clapboard Queen Anne with wooden shutters painted red. I don't think my own child lay in bed at night mentally rearranging dollhouse furniture as I had once done, but she played with that house and she played hard. Strange new dolls and out-of-scale items were always being added. I sometimes joined her and tried to contribute my own aesthetic finesse. "Shall we pick tiny flowering weeds and arrange dollhouse bouquets in upside-down china thimbles? Shall I glue strips of lace to the window tops for curtains?" When we moved from Florida to Pennsylvania, the dollhouse was given its own special moving crate, constructed around it in our seashell-stuccoed home and carefully removed once we arrived at our redbrick

farmhouse. But daughters grow quickly, and the dollhouse was carried down to the basement not long after. I imagined we might carry it up again when my youngest child and second daughter was old enough, but she never showed any affinity for miniature worlds, preferring her own magic world where she, with a unicorn horn glued to her headband, waved rainbow streamers and galloped with flying ponies.

I sometimes remembered my child's dollhouse while I lay in bed trying to fall asleep. I would picture the sheet-draped lump in the corner of our dirt-floor basement and imagine uncovering it, repairing it, maybe repainting those red shutters green. Only now my own house is an 1880 farmhouse where the plaster keeps failing in new places and the wood floors we have yet to refinish give us frequent splinters. Glue guns are no use against the immensity of its perennial decay. Of course this real, right-sized house must take precedence over a toy. What kind of fool paints tiny doll shutters when her own shutters need a good scrub and a new paint job? When the planks of her own front porch are once again rotting through? And so, as needed, I paint the walls, my husband measures wallpaper, we bring in helpers for the really big jobs. Whereas my daughter's house had only two tiny terra-cotta pots filled with felt roses on the front porch, I keep adding new garden areas to our property and then feeling overwhelmed by the upkeep. The work of making this Pennsylvania home has always felt beyond us, but it has also buoyed us. It is right and good to make a place better and more beautiful.

Home repairs in an old house can feel unending. Scratch one to-do from your list, and three more are added. And yet somehow over this past decade, we made enough progress to invite my husband's parents to live with us. A few years ago, in early summer, they put their own Texas home on the market. In July, they sold it. In September, they moved into the guest barn that sits just beyond our kitchen door. In October, my father-in-law's health declined. In November, he died here, at our Pennsylvania home, and we realized that he would not use the woodworking tools we had arranged in a shed for him. He would not attend his grandson's Eagle Scout ceremony or his granddaughter's high school graduation. And he would never know that I had uncovered the dollhouse and moved it to a folding table. He would never know that I had plugged in a task lamp in that corner of the basement. He would never see the dollhouse repair supplies I had already gathered, things like new wallpaper with miniature patterns and a dollhouse electrical kit with light bulbs right-sized for mice.

Home repair is my family legacy. Building and beautifying are sacred work. As a child I sensed this. My parents may not have spoken of it, but they demonstrated how much it mattered. It wasn't enough to open our Bibles and invite people into our homes. We must also vacuum the floors. Wallpaper our walls. Build decks and grow flowers. We do this for love of others, but we also do this simply for love: love for the God who made this earth to be our home, love for others, love for self, and love for the beauty of this given world. It is easy to tell myself that my fascination with miniatures was simply the child-sized version of the work I watched my parents do, as if I were "playing house" and in some way practicing for adult life. But if dollhouses are childish things, they are childish things I feel compelled to take up again.

Building and beautifying are sacred work.

This year when the garden goes back to sleep, the evenings draw in, and the temperature outside is too cold for new paint, I intend to take myself to the snug stone-walled basement. I will finally remove the sheet, turn on the task lamp, and plug in my glue gun. I will tell myself that a grandchild might play with this house one day, and while true, this is not really the reason for the work. The reason is that miniature worlds are marvels that help us marvel at the right-sized world again. Loving and losing over a lifetime can take the shine off ordinary life. Making and unmaking and remaking a home can take a toll. I have grown weary. I have lost touch with wonder. But I once learned to care for houses and gardens and cakes and kittens by holding them in my hands. I need to hold these things in my hands again, cup them entirely in my palm, like God holding me, like God holding the whole world in his hands.

I first learned to be a placemaker in the dollhouse my father made for me. Tiny shingles and carpets and thimbles full of pretty weeds once inspired my love for making and tending a home. I am a placemaker and a homekeeper on a larger scale now. I once counted inches but now count in feet and yards and acres. Yet I feel I am overdue for a return to my childhood comforts, the source of my love for home. The past few years, we have weathered the loss of some we love, the upheaval of major home repairs, a pandemic, and the tumult of growing up with our teens. I am tired. I am grateful. I find myself feeling both a little lost and determined to press on. I think I will find my bearings by reacquainting myself with the comfort of tiny, homely things. I will grow small in order to come home again.

ROOTS
& SKY
A Journey Home in Four Seasons
RISTIE PURIFOY

Inspiration

House Books for Children (and the Child in Us)

Before I ever bought a tiny chair or had a dollhouse of my own, I learned to love houses and interiors through picture books and illustrated chapter books. These are some of my favorites then and now. When I turn the pages of these books, I remember what a house can be, and I am filled with new energy for the task of making my own home.

Brambly Hedge books

written and illustrated by Jill Barklem

These exquisite little books with intricate painted illustrations tell seasonal stories about a community of mice living in an English hedgerow. The interiors are stunning and full of beautiful details. I once fell in love with a patchwork tea cozy I spotted in a Brambly Hedge cottage home. I'm determined to have something like it one day for my own Brown Betty teapot.

A Time to Keep: The Tasha Tudor Book of Holidays

written and illustrated by Tasha Tudor

Though ostensibly a book of old-fashioned seasonal celebrations, all of Tudor's work offers inspiring glimpses of everyday domestic life in the nineteenth century.

The Borrowers

written by Mary Norton, illustrated by Beth and Joe Krush

This entire series was one of the great loves of my childhood. Tiny people create their own homes by "borrowing" items from us. Spools of thread become tables and stools, thimbles are cups, handkerchiefs become bedsheets, and on and on in clever, creative ways that helped me see ordinary objects with eyes of wonder.

Let's Go Home: The Wonderful Things About a House

written by Cynthia Rylant, illustrated by Wendy Anderson Halperin

All of Rylant's books were favorites when I was raising my own young children, and I still love to return to them today. This one celebrates the life that is lived in each room of a house with marvelous, surprising, detailed illustrations. Books can remind us of the loveliness of our own ordinary lives. This one does that for me.

Farmhouse

written and illustrated by Sophie Blackall

Published only a few years ago, this picture book is a work of art. Based on a real house and family, it shows the dollhouse-like world that once nurtured a family with twelve children.

Party Place

I do not think anyone can keep a house well who will not acknowledge the poetry of place. Humans may have built the very first house because they needed shelter from sun and wind and rain, but we have gone on building houses and caring for houses because a house is a vessel for life. It not only keeps the sun off and the damp out but gives meaning to our days. Language becomes poetry when it offers both a literal meaning on its surface and a figurative meaning down in its depths. Like a poem, a house holds our experiences in such a way that we can probe their deeper significance. A house is not like an hourglass. Minutes do not filter through our homes like sand through our fingers. Rather, a house catches time, holding it, forming it, slowing it. If you doubt me, if you insist like a scientist that every second is like every other, then I invite you to help me set the table for a birthday party at Maplehurst.

Here are the rainbow-striped birthday candles for the cake. I found them on a high pantry shelf buried in a pale yellow Blue Bell ice cream container where I keep cupcake liners and the cookie cutters that refuse to fit in the baking drawer. While digging around for them, I also found a candle in the shape of the number two. Was it used for Lily's twelfth birthday? Or for Elsa's second? I can't say with certainty, but a steady trickle of birthday party memories bubble up in my mind. I remember spreading a birthday picnic for Beau, the younger son who had been born to us in early spring. We laid our picnic quilt beneath a cloud of white cherry blossoms. The food was simple, but we could

A house catches time, holding it, forming it, slowing it.

not have purchased finer party decorations in any shop. On my own first birthday at Maplehurst, when a bit of humidity in the air announced the shift from spring to summer, the older son with whom I share a birthday joined me for a birthday portrait on the top of a sleeping giant. One of the old maple trees along the driveway had fallen in the night. Before heading out to canoe the Brandywine River, we climbed the trunk to pose together. I had to pull Thad up beside me because his little legs couldn't quite make the leap.

I reach for dessert plates next and wonder whether to choose the white china Jonathan and I received as wedding gifts, the floral-patterned ironstone I bought secondhand, or the blue-and-white china my father bought in Japan during his Army days before he had even met my mother. My parents recently downsized in order to make their home with my younger brother, his wife, and their five children, and when I first unwrapped the blue-and-white china my mother was passing on to me, I remembered how the petite, shallow bowls—about the size of my palm—held my father's favorite banana pudding after countless family dinners. I never have set the table for a memorable occasion without finding myself a little lost in time.

Twelve years ago, we brought a birthday party with us when we moved from Florida to Pennsylvania. We were scheduled to sign the closing papers for our home purchase on August 1, only a few weeks before our oldest child would turn nine, and I felt confident of two things. One, I would not have the time or energy to plan a birthday party in my ninth month of pregnancy while unpacking boxes. And two, a birthday party would be vital for the daughter beginning third grade in a new school. I wanted her to be able to hand out party invitations to every girl in her new class, almost like old-fashioned calling cards, which meant settling on a birthday party theme and creating those invitations while we still called Florida home. When our moving van was fully loaded and the back doors locked, it held cardboard boxes labeled *baby girl clothes* for the fourth child kicking away in my belly, and two plastic bins marked *birthday party*. Unbeknownst to us, it also contained the Pixar *Cars*–themed Lightning McQueen pajamas my younger son and third child insisted on wearing to bed every night. Our family's move to Pennsylvania would be set to the music of a three-year-old's grief for his lost pajamas.

The flower-fairy tea party we hosted on our new front porch that September has remained one of the birthday celebrations I remember most

clearly, though that could be because I went into labor with my second daughter and fourth child three days later. We've updated our wooden porch since then, removing the gingerbread railings that obscured the home's plain Quaker origins, but when I think of my firstborn's ninth birthday tea party, I remember how the white-painted porch railings perfectly framed the glass-topped table we'd brought with us from Florida. I remember how we strung fabric bunting in shades of pink from the railings and draped pastel-colored candy necklaces—just like the ones my father used to buy for me and my sisters—around the edges of a glass trifle dish ready to be plucked and worn by our small guests. I can still feel how the warm, sticky air of summer blew out in a rush of autumn rain. By the time we cut the blackberry-topped birthday cake, we had moved the party from the porch to the dining room. Our need for shelter from the storm meant that we baptized two spaces with our first celebration. The weather was turning. The shape of our family was shifting. Soon we would be six.

Traditions

Birthday Teacups

My firstborn's flower-fairy tea party began a new birthday tradition for my daughters. That was the year I gave her the gift of a china teacup and saucer, bought secondhand. It had occurred to me that year that if I gave her a new teacup every birthday until she graduated high school, she'd have a mismatched set of ten to call her own. The next year, I gave her baby sister a miniature china cup painted with the image of Hunca Munca the mouse from Beatrix Potter's book about the dollhouse.

Today, my shelves hold Lily's ten teacups and another ten for Elsa. I made sure to photograph each daughter with her cup each year to help us keep track. Finding cups on eBay or Etsy with meaningful details like asters (September's flower) or ladybugs (recalling one daughter's infant nickname) always felt like a special triumph, a way of slowing time and anticipating a fruitful future for my September girls.

Sleepover Room

You could say that Maplehurst is the house of my dreams with its narrow back stairs and spacious front porch. And yet I rarely dream about this house. In my dreams, I almost always visit the houses of my childhood. There is the small brick bungalow on busy Jersey Street, my family's first home in Texas, and there is the elegant contemporary home where I spent so many schoolday afternoons and weekends. From the street, that house looked like any beautiful suburban brick home. In the back, it was a long sheet of glass with a view of the woods. I remember raking leaves in those woods and being paid a dime for each garbage bag we filled. I'm sorry now to remember how we not only raked the leaves from the paths but also enthusiastically pulled them from the woods, eager to fill more bags and earn more dimes.

That glass-walled house belonged to my childhood best friend. Molly had dark hair and pale, freckled skin, and we met on the first day of kindergarten in Mrs. Smith's classroom. I shared a bedroom with my younger sisters, and my mother refused to buy Barbie dolls, which may explain why sleepovers and playdates with Molly almost always took place in her family's home. She had her own bedroom and was the proud caretaker of Barbie's Dreamhouse and a shelf full of Cabbage Patch dolls. Forty-two years have passed since I met my first friend, but I can still mentally walk through every room of her home, and at night, while I sleep, I frequently do.

The floors in the public rooms were tiled with large ceramic squares. They were cool underfoot, but the accent rugs were soft and thick. In the dining room, a full wall of glass-fronted cabinets held a collection of colorful antique porcelain. Molly told me which pieces would be hers one day and which pieces would belong to her sister, and

I wished for bits of old china with my name on them, though I wasn't even sure I liked the fussy curlicues and gilded accents on this collection. I suppose because we were so young, we also spent a lot of time playing in her parents' bedroom and especially their walk-in closet. The closet epitomized the things I loved most about Molly's home: it was always clean and tidy and organized. In that house, I felt sure that any need could be met. It was quiet too. Unlike me, my friend had no baby brother, and I don't remember ever seeing a houseguest. The grandfather who once lived in the back bedroom had died before I began my visits—he lived on only in the few memories my friend shared with me. At Molly's house, we were alone, and the only interruption to our play came when her mother padded quietly into the room with snacks neatly laid out on Tupperware trays.

My own home today probably has more in common with the noisy, somewhat chaotic place my parents made together. Children, animals, drop-in friends, and overnight guests. Homegrown flowers dripping petals and pollen on every table. Ours is a busy, bustling place like the one I grew up in, and yet when I bring my youngest child and her best friend a tray of sliced fruit after school, I always think of Molly's mom. When a visiting child or teenager notices and comments on something my own kids have long ago stopped seeing—"Your home is beautiful, Mrs. Purifoy! Your flowers are so pretty!"—I wonder if they are feeling something like what I used to feel at my friend's house. I hope so. I hope even if they visit only once, they take with them an expanded vision of what a home can be.

I had so many sleepovers with Molly over the years that I can recall sleeping in almost every room of her house. Most often, I suppose, we slept in her room. Molly would take the white metal daybed, and I would sleep on the pullout trundle. If we were watching a movie, we usually slept in the back bedroom off the kitchen, the one that once belonged to her grandfather, but I can also remember blankets laid on the cool tiles

I know that childhood is short, that friendships thrive in comfortable places, and that sometimes mothers pour all of our love into neat apple slices and tumblers of milk and fresh sheets on the bed because sometimes that's all we can do.

of the living room floor—and one memorable night when we slept in her parents' bedroom and my friend found a scary movie on the television. I scrunched my eyes shut when she refused to click away, but the music was enough to give me nightmares for weeks. My friend was always more of the risk-taker. The one to seek out new experiences. The one in a hurry to grow up. I still grieve the reality that she never got the chance.

Maybe that's why I created the sleepover room at Maplehurst. I know that childhood is short, that friendships thrive in comfortable places, and that sometimes mothers pour all of our love into neat apple slices and tumblers of milk and fresh sheets on the bed because sometimes that's all we can do. That's all we can control. Children may still find scary movies and fast cars, but in addition to prayer I offer up this small third-floor bedroom with its sloping attic roof, bright floral wallpaper, and two white metal daybeds with pullout trundles underneath. There is no television in this room, but there is a closet with baskets of old toys and a small bookshelf with some of my favorites: Nancy Drew, Laura Ingalls, *The Baby-Sitters' Club*. Four children can sleep in this room. We've hosted cousins, my own four children slept up there together a few years in a row on Christmas Eve, and even though my older son has lately filled the room with his LEGO creations, I already have this space earmarked for grandchildren and their friends. I hope this is the room some middle-aged woman will visit one day in her dreams. I hope this is the room she remembers when she remembers that she was loved.

Inspiration

Choosing Toys

There is no reason the beauty of a home should compete with the needs of children. Houses were places of wonder for me when I was a girl, and I am still inspired by those memories. Whether or not you live with children, or hope to one day, considering your place from a child's point of view can help you bring more comfort and even whimsy into your home.

When we had bookshelves made for our front room, we asked the carpenter if he could also build a window seat in the dining room's bay window. When I was a girl, I loved bay windows with built-in seats and always wanted one of my own for reading and daydreaming. Our new window seat is a dream come true even if I am too grown to curl up on it. Still, I pull my reading chair as near as I can and sometimes a child joins me there.

My mother didn't object to Barbie on aesthetic grounds—I think she simply preferred the innocence of a baby doll for her daughters—but I can understand why my friend's Barbie Dreamhouse lived in a corner of her bedroom and not in the family's elegant living room. Children's toys are not always beautiful, but we can make more thoughtful choices, especially when it comes to the smaller toys that will get carried around. Though plastic may be inexpensive, cheap toys have a way of piling up and getting tossed. Toys made of natural materials cost more, but they make beautiful decor and can be handed down to the next sibling, or even the next generation. Far be it from me to shame anyone for a plastic dollhouse like the one I once loved, but giving our children beautiful, carefully crafted toys as we are able is one more way to love them well. It is one more way we can find comfort in the act of comforting them.

A Quilted Sky

This morning, I drove our pickup truck to the garden center in search of deals on late-season plants. Fall is the best time for planting, not least because so many items are marked half off. I only drive the truck if I am plant shopping, preferring the backup camera in our minivan and a sound system that connects directly to my phone. In the truck, radio is the only option, which is how I accidentally heard a devastating story about six children from one family lost in a wartime bombing of their apartment building. They are only six of thousands, but numbers are different from names. Why some children are born into violence and some into flourishing peace I cannot say, but when I turned off the radio, I thought about my own childhood. There were no bombs, only blanket forts and a game in which the wall-to-wall carpet in our family's den became hot lava. My sisters and I loved to play out disaster scenarios. Perhaps it reminded us that we were safe.

The family home of our earliest childhood was very small, yet somehow we craved even smaller spaces. It may be that children share the instincts of vulnerable burrowing creatures. We could not dig tunnels underground, no matter how we longed for cozy dens like the ones in a Beatrix Potter book, but we could throw a blanket over the dining room table and make our home underneath. Sometimes we needed three quilts to do the job properly, but if our mother was not expecting guests, we three girls could live under the table quite happily for a week with our dolls and our snacks and the small headlamps we had found in our Christmas stockings one year.

I can't recall the last time I sat beneath a quilted sky, but blankets still bring me comfort. All these years later, I feel a sense of security each September when I fold away the light linen throws of summer and pull out a stack of blankets in fleece and wool. Colder days are coming, but I feel prepared to welcome them. Lately, blankets and patchwork quilts have become a design inspiration as well. After my mother-in-law moved out, our Black Barn became again a guesthouse and a gathering place for teenagers. It was in need of fresh style and warmth, but I struggled to find the inspiration I needed to guide my choices. Decorating my house feels easy. The English-country-house style of intense color, pattern, and beautiful clutter has always felt right for this stately farmhouse. William Morris wallpaper, a pair of Staffordshire china dogs, a soft and deep rolled-arm sofa: these items are all obvious choices for my house. But what about a barn? The rustic wood and peeling paint of primitive style would be a clear possibility, but those things have never made my own heart sing. I like color and pretty, mismatched china, and while I love the scent as well as the look of the knotty pine barn walls, I knew that all that barn wood could use a great deal of softening. My friend and houseguest Kristin came to my rescue. "You should look for quilts," she said. "Old, colorful quilts."

Somehow that one word unlocked something in me. Maybe it's because I've always kept the patchwork quilt my great-grandmother made for me when I was a baby in Texas, maybe it's because of all my years of blanket-fort play, or maybe it's because I now live near so many incredible Amish-country quilters, but the words were hardly out of Kristin's mouth before I was off—to eBay and Etsy and Facebook Marketplace, and even my local thrift and antique stores. At first, I felt a little overwhelmed by the choices. So many quilts looked like burgundy and hunter green relics of the early 1990s or dusty pink and country blue remnants of the 1980s, but then I started noticing the Dresden patterned quilts. They featured bright wheels of color against crisp white or creamy ivory. They offered a soft, old-fashioned comfort, but they were somehow modern too. I had found my inspiration.

One Sunday after church, Jonathan and I drove up into the foothills northwest of Philadelphia to pick up a Dresden quilt with a bright green grid on creamy white with multicolored fabric wheels. When we brought it home, I found it topped the queen-size guest bed perfectly. A few days later, I discovered online a small colorful quilt in something called the Crown of Thorns pattern. The name is somber, but the colors are cheerful pinks and greens and yellows. It is the right size for a wall hanging, but I have tossed it over the end of a pale blue thrifted sofa with soft down-filled cushions. Finally, I realized that the large bare portion of wall where I had been trying to hang a gallery of small framed prints was really asking for one large hanging quilt. I found a simple one in white

Quilts can be art. Quilts can hold memories. Quilts can offer a safe sky over our heads and our childhoods.

and turquoise, and now it looks a little something like modern art in a scale that makes sense for a soaring lofted barn.

Quilts can be art. Quilts can hold memories. Quilts can offer a safe sky over our heads and our childhoods. That some homes will be ruined by war or destroyed by floods seems to me all the more reason to fill the ones we have with things of beauty and comfort. The making of shelter is as instinctual for us as it is for other animals. Children know this. We know it, too, if we listen to our hearts. To make a home, and make it well, is to build a wall against chaos. Not every wall will hold fast forever, but creating a space of well-ordered beauty is a task worth doing for the whole of one's life. It is one way of living a life of prayer. It is one way of praying that every child might know the security of a bright quilted sky.

Thrifting

Quilts

There is a great deal I do not know about quilts, but one thing I learned very quickly is that not all quilts with hand-stitching are handmade. Like anything else with widespread appeal, hand-stitched quilts have been sent out en masse from factories. You can usually spot the pretenders. The hand-applied stitches are large and often a bit careless, but quilts are warm and comforting whether stitched by a local Amish grandmother or an employee in a fabric mill. Authenticity matters only if it matters to you. The grandchildren who picnic on your quilt will not be bothered.

With quilts, or any vintage items, you decide what matters most to you. Is it color? Pattern? Age? One of my favorite quilts has colors that seem to perfectly straddle the 1980s and '90s. The binding is burgundy, and the most prominent colors are dusty rose, mint green, and powder blue. These are almost exactly the colors of the bedroom I decorated for myself in 1989, which means I have a nostalgic fondness for them that is impervious to fashion. Sure enough, there is a cross-stitched label on my quilt that says it was made by Twila Ward in August 1989. *Thank you,* Twila.

This also seems like the right moment to tell you about my favorite quilt-centric childhood memory. Better even than blanket forts were the indoor picnics our mother spread for us on the floor of the family den. Whether it was too hot in summer or too rainy in winter, an indoor picnic—with a quilt on the floor and our plastic lunch boxes neatly filled—transformed ordinary food into a memorable, movable feast. *Thank you,* Mom.

Sick Days

I was a sickly child, though I didn't know it. Perhaps it was because my mother told me stories of her own difficult asthmatic childhood in the days before nebulizers and the pills she would break into chocolate pudding for me that my sense of what counted as good health became a little skewed. My mother's childhood asthma had often sent her to the hospital, while mine generally just sent me home from gym class. Still, some of my most vivid memories in my childhood home on Jersey Street take me back to days when I was sick. I remember recovering from chicken pox in my parents' large bed with a tray for chicken noodle soup on one side and the missed schoolwork my teacher had sent home with my sister on the other. I remember other sick days when my mother made a special cushioned nest for me on the rocking couch in our den with its granny-square afghan thrown across the back. Our family television was in that room, but I remember the frustration of finding only soap operas playing during the day. I would check all of the channels before returning to *The Borrowers* by Mary Norton. Research has shown that humans tend to make more memories from negative or even traumatic experiences than we do from positive events. And yet I also remember childhood illnesses for the goodness and coziness of a day spent at home: soft blankets on the couch, extra attention from my mother, and a comforting sense that I was floating in time while the world rushed on without me.

We cannot speak of houses as shelters or havens without assuming harsh realities. To call our home a sanctuary is to acknowledge a world of danger. And yet each of these words suggests that we are hiding. At times, we do need to hide, if only for a night and a few hours of excellent sleep, but homes offer more than just reprieve or escape. Homes are also for healing. A healing home might look a little different for everyone, but for me as a child, it felt like a soft bed, it tasted like soup from a can with saltine crackers on the side, and it smelled like menthol and fresh-baked chocolate chip cookies. A healing home need not be fancy or an out-of-reach ideal.

A healing home isn't only necessary for days when we are sick. It is a daily necessity—a daily grace—for people who are seeking to love the world and their neighbors well. Loving others will call us out into difficult places and relationships and endeavors, but when we find our hearts (and perhaps also our nervous systems) a little worse for wear, home—with its scents and flavors and familiar comforts—can heal like little else. It can heal us, and it can heal those who live with us. It can heal guests and even occasional visitors. Our word *heal* is related to the word *whole*. In a sense, to be healed is to be made whole. A healing home helps integrate all the parts of ourselves. If the world has knocked us out of balance, home can set us right again. This means that a healing home must address not only the body but the mind, the heart, and the soul as well.

Perhaps because I have such fond memories of childhood sick days, "taking to my bed" is something I still practice as a busy wife and mother. I have a highly sensitive nervous system and a propensity to allergies and asthma, which means that I can quickly reach a state of over-stimulated exhaustion. The result of that has often been an

If the world has knocked us out of balance, home can set us right again.

extended bout with bronchitis. Thankfully, I have learned how to retreat within my own noisy home and busy life in order to lessen the likelihood of an extended sickness. My kind husband knows there will be days I need to go to bed in the middle of the afternoon. Thankfully, he is an extrovert who finds himself energized at a dinner table with our four children, and I like to think that when he brings me dinner in bed before tiptoeing back down to that chaotic kitchen, our children are learning that even parents need and deserve care. I hope they will always know that they need and deserve care. I hope they give that care. I hope they receive that care.

Traumatic memories may stick like glue, but I have found that memories of caregiving do the same. Some of the most precious memories I have made in this home are memories of caring for my own sick children. Though I do have a sadly long list of traumatic memories involving emergency rooms and EpiPens, and one really unfortunate summer we still refer to as the summer of the rabies shots, I also remember holding a feverish baby girl who would nap only on my shoulder. I remember carrying lunch trays up to bedrooms with food I hoped would tempt someone's appetite. I remember nights I held a well-wrapped toddler on my lap as we rocked on the front porch. Twenty minutes in a steamy bathroom followed by twenty minutes in the cold night air is sometimes all it takes to heal a touch of croup. Even now, my youngest will sometimes say, "Mom, do you remember when you used to carry me outside at night? Do you remember how we saw the stars?"

"Of course I remember," I tell her. *Of course I remember the brilliant silver lining on those sleepless, fearful nights.*

The Healing Home

A healing home makes space for medicine and a cool-mist humidifier, but it might also prioritize a fresh box of crayons or a sun-warmed towel straight from the clothesline. A healing home can help our physical bodies and inspire our creativity. A healing home can restore our strength and might even contribute to healing the planet. We must never underestimate the power and the reach of a healing home.

Here are some of our favorite traditions for making a home that can heal:

- A spoonful of local honey at bedtime for coughs (for children older than two)
- Making a nest-like bed on the couch
- An essential oil diffuser
- A hot water bottle with a knitted or felted cover
- An electric blanket for my own winter bed (dual temperature controls are highly recommended if you do not sleep alone)
- A convenient basket filled with seasonal picture books or prayer books
- A record player for listening to some of your favorite tunes and melodies
- A spot for seasonal treasures (like acorns in autumn or daffodils in spring) to connect us and our home to the rhythms of the natural world
- A large stack of cloth napkins for everyday use
- An electric teakettle for boiling water without turning on the stove
- Bulk spices in glass jars for making real chai tea in winter
- Straw hats and sun hats hung by the back door in summer
- Pretty hanging baskets in the kitchen: one for mail and one for receipts
- Real cotton handkerchiefs
- Seasonal simmer pots on the stove (simmer water with scented additions like orange peel and a cinnamon stick)
- A puzzle board with an in-process puzzle (especially in winter)
- Children's toys that do not make noise

The Castle Under the Tree

The first thing my husband built at Maplehurst was a bin for garden compost. I watched him work from our bedroom window while I fed and rocked our baby. The compost bin had two big bays built of wood, one for fresh waste and one for almost-ready compost. I can still remember the boys' excitement while their dad sketched his plans and pulled out his tools. I don't think they knew what compost was, but they relished the noise of the power saw and collected the scrap wood for their play. The second thing Jonathan built was a castle-themed tree house around the trunk of an enormous Norway spruce. The drooping branches were the castle roof, and two white flags flapped in the breeze from corner posts on either side of an opening in the fortress walls. To connect the opening with the ground, he built a short ladder even a three-year-old boy could climb. I remember thinking, *A compost pile? A castle? Are these really our priorities right now?* I felt both irritated and unsure. Maybe these *were* our priorities, but we hadn't discussed it. If we had, I'm not sure what I would have said. I'd been dreaming of making a spacious place for our young family, but my mind was so preoccupied with needs—of house and children—I hardly knew where to begin.

Twelve years on, I can say with certainty that such things were not the most pressing needs of our new place. The old limestone mortar around our bricks was failing, our original wooden windows were rotting, and most of the shutters were missing at least some of their slats. If my husband had been smarter but less wise, he would have focused on these larger repairs and projects. Thankfully, he was ruled by a husband's and a father's love, hence the

Sometimes placemakers must be practical. But sometimes good placemakers must also build castles in the trees.

compost bins I would fill with garden and kitchen waste for years and the castle where two little boys shape-shifted from knights to Robin Hood. Eventually the tree grew too large for the hole in the castle floor and the whole structure was torn down, but by then the boys had grown so tall they didn't need the ladder to step inside, and the Robin Hood hat and vest no longer fit either of them.

I can hardly remember what our house looked like before we tuck-pointed the brick and repaired the windows. Repairs like that are often invisible because they simply restore something to the state it should be. No one who visits this house exclaims that the paint on the wooden windowsills is not flaking and the wood is not rotting away. I must take care or I, too, will forget what was and thus forget to give thanks for what is. But the compost bins and the castle around the tree are vivid in my memory, the wood Jonathan used to make them still fresh and sweet-smelling in my mind. The blue lions painted on those white flags still have a three-year-old's fingerprints around their edges. It doesn't matter at all that these things are no longer here, but it matters a great deal that they once were.

I wish I could tell my twelve-years-younger self that everything would work out. I wish I could tell her not to worry so much about priorities and simply live. Simply rest. Simply watch those boys play, and give thanks. I wanted to do and make and create. I wanted to beat back the disorder and insist on beauty, but I was tired and struggling to nurse a newborn. In the swirl of our first autumn in the farmhouse, it sometimes seemed as if my family members were the reasons I could make little progress in creating the family home I'd been dreaming of for years. But my husband had his priorities right. He understood that these little boys would not be little for long. He understood that solid windows give one kind of comfort and play castles another.

Sometimes placemakers must be practical. We must postpone the kitchen redesign and call in the plaster repairman or the electrician. We must budget for new storm windows and set aside our plans for a new sofa. We keep a close eye on that budget but only until the chimney sweep tells us our chimney liner has a rusty hole in it and must be replaced before winter. Then we take the plunge and do what must be done. But sometimes good placemakers must also build castles in the trees. These are not at all like castles in the sky, for they remain real and solid and meaningful long after they have disappeared.

A List of Things You Will Not Regret

- The time you spent on the floor playing Candy Land with a little boy who cheated by looking at the cards
- The unique color-coded built-in storage bin system you created in the boys' closet for their vast LEGO collection (it's okay that the bins now hold socks and hair gel and that one inappropriate T-shirt your younger son bought at the thrift store that you will not allow him to wear)
- The galaxy you strained your neck painting on their bedroom ceiling
- The height marker for your children and their visiting cousins handwritten on the kitchen wall
- The Sharpie marker scribbles on the second-floor landing made by a toddler with artistic ambitions
- Painting the trim in the corner bedroom pink even though the daughter moved out and the son moved in before you could finish the paint job
- Asking your sons to repaint the kitchen siding even though the concrete patio has a bit of paint now too

You won't regret the time. You won't regret the money. You won't regret the effort. Because you won't—you absolutely will not—regret the love.

Playing House

I have a friend who is quite serious about her work and has a tendency toward perfectionism. Apparently, her therapist advised her she needed to learn how to play. When she told me this, I immediately wondered whether I knew how to play. I can be quite serious myself. I'm a thinker, prone to melancholy. But then I remembered my long-ago dollhouse and understood with a rush of gratitude that my house is where I play. And it always has been that way for me. When I filled a silver thimble with the tiniest flowers I could find and placed it on the doll's dining room table, I wasn't practicing for adulthood. I was playing. Today, when I gather up the dahlias I have grown and arrange their sunset colors in my thrifted silver pitcher, I become creatively absorbed in my own self-directed activity. What I am doing doesn't matter to anyone but me. It makes no tangible difference to the world, yet it makes me feel alive, as if some burden I didn't know I carried had suddenly dropped from my shoulders.

Play is inherently unproductive. A waste of time. It feels trivial. And this is why it is so good for us. When we play, our minds are at rest. Our spirits are replenished. When we play, we are reminded that time was not given to us to "use" but to live. And if we have no time for delight, are we really living? I love that word *delight* because it seems to assume some object. Happiness and joy might simply be, but delight suggests some *thing*: the taste of June strawberries, the musical chime of our grandfather clock, the way winter sunlight dances across the kitchen wall every sunny afternoon.

Those who study such things tell us that a child's play always has rules. These rules are internal, individual, and idiosyncratic, but they give structure to the activity. Here is one of my rules, borrowed from a wise friend: first, *shop your house*. Myquillyn Smith, known

as "The Nester" in her many books, coined this phrase[1] and helped me prioritize something I vaguely knew to do: before clicking *buy* or heading to a store, refresh and rearrange your home using things you already own. It's incredible how often the perfect solution is found lying in a closet or sitting awkwardly in some corner of the house. After we built a window seat in our dining room, I found pink linen throw pillows in an old wardrobe. They had never looked quite right in the parlor, but they were just what I needed to cushion the new seat.

Once I've "shopped" the house, my second rule for house play is *don't buy new when you can thrift*. This one requires discipline, but discipline is much easier to come by when it feels like it's part of a game. Online shopping has become ubiquitous, and big-box stores have learned how to bring the very latest styles to shoppers at bargain prices, but years of homemaking have taught me that disappointment and an endless cycle of buying and throwing away often follows the purchase of something new. While it's tempting to solve a decorating dilemma with an impulse buy, I have found that waiting for just the right vintage items to show up at the thrift store or in an online listing can be incredibly satisfying. The most beautiful pieces in my home are inevitably the ones I've waited for.

I've decided that learning to play and prioritizing my own playfully creative activities is one more way to grow younger inside even as my body

ages. I have long assumed that the moments of joyful self-absorption I recall from my childhood are available only to children. The good news is that we can become like children again, and our homes can help nudge us in that direction. I wonder now if it was harder to be childlike when I was raising young children. My joy in those days came as I witnessed their play. The summer my youngest and a small crowd of little neighbors created a whole village of shops selling pine cones and pebbles and foraged berries in the shaded corner of our property beneath the old Norway spruce trees almost made me feel as if I were a child again. Now that my children are nearly grown, it is up to me to keep play alive in this place. I like to think that play keeps a house young at heart too. For houses respond not only to the craftsmanship of wood restoration and plaster repair but also to the child who scratches the name of her tooth fairy into the glass pane of her bedroom window. To the mother who keeps growing and bringing in flowers, though tomatoes and carrots would be much more practical. And to the father who tosses circles of pizza dough so high they nearly touch the kitchen's old paneled ceiling.

I like to think that play keeps a house young at heart too. For houses respond not only to the craftsmanship of wood restoration and plaster repair but also to the child who scratches the name of her tooth fairy into the glass pane of her bedroom window.

THE GIFT OF GATHERING DOUCETTE
THE DIY STYLE FINDER
COZY MINIMALIST HOME
CHERYL MENDELSON
HOME COMFORTS
OLD HOUSES NASH
MARTHA STEWART'S NEW OLD HOUSE
FARM ANATOMY JULIA ROTHMAN
THE GIFT OF HOME DOUCETTE
THE GIFT OF GATHERING DOUCETTE
BEAUTY BY DESIGN CURTIS
A LOVELY LIFE
SEEDTIME and HARVEST CHRISTIE PURIFOY
A HOME in bloom CHRISTIE PURIFOY
GARDEN MAKER CHRISTIE PURIFOY
THE COUNTRY DIARY OF AN EDWARDIAN LADY Edith Holden
THE GIFT OF GATHERING PLANNER
The Pre-Raphaelite Language of Flowers
THE NESTING PLACE
COZY MINIMALIST HOME
WELCOME HOME
the creative family
GREER

Botanicum

National Parks
WORLD ATLAS OF NATIONS

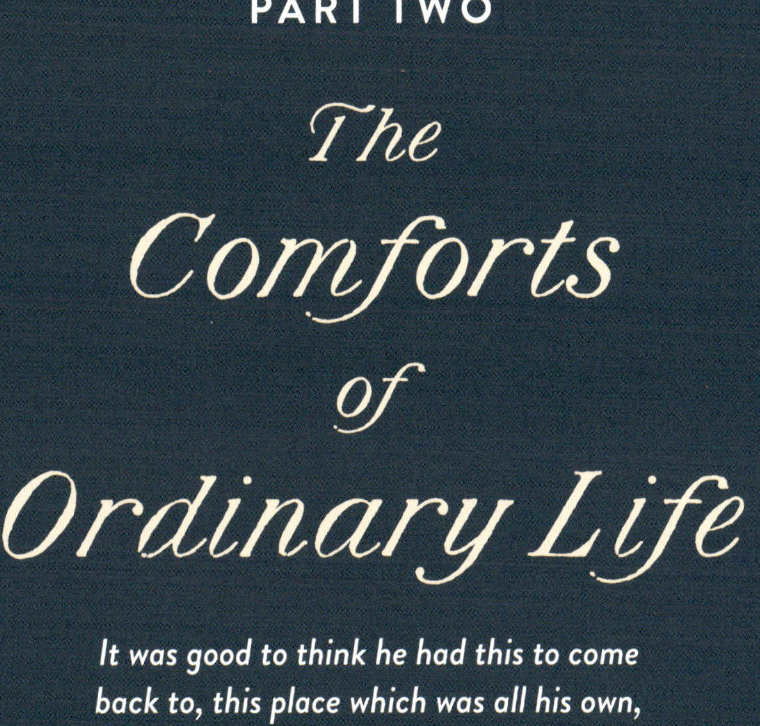

PART TWO

The Comforts of Ordinary Life

It was good to think he had this to come back to, this place which was all his own, these things which were so glad to see him again and could always be counted upon for the same simple welcome.

KENNETH GRAHAME,
THE WIND IN THE WILLOWS

When Wanderers Become Pilgrims

In Florida, we were wanderers. Despite the fact that we were homeowners enjoying our first real backyard with the kids, we were unable to sink our roots into the ground of that place. It felt as if we lived on the surface of things, and I was profoundly aware of a lack of purpose to our days. It felt as if we were biding our time, but for what? Till our children had grown? Till retirement and downsizing and travel? I wanted these child-raising years to have more meaning than that. I hoped they would add up to something more than simply time spent. Gradually, leaning into these hard-to-articulate desires, we understood that whatever dreams we began to dream, they would be realized in some other place. Florida was temporary shelter, like a tent in the desert, but the palm trees and beaches and neighborhood pools of our oasis were beautiful, and we rested there.

Maplehurst transformed us from wanderers to pilgrims. Calling this house home meant that we would journey in place while the seasons shifted overhead. The signs of our progression would come as drifting snow was followed by magnolia blossoms and by the sometimes gradual and occasionally sudden advance of the height markers we began to pencil on the frame of the kitchen door. Humans were made to journey through life, not wander, which is the only explanation for the fact that we prefer the rigors of pilgrimage to the indolence of the wilderness. In Florida, my primary task was to sit near the pool with an eye on the kids, and yet I chafed at that easy life. In Pennsylvania, we were overwhelmed at the tasks before us—raising four children, repairing an old house, welcoming guests—and yet our worry was shot through with joy. Now we could see a path extending to a far horizon. Now we talked constantly of all that we wanted for this home, for this place, for these people in our care. Now our roots stretched painfully down and down and again down some more.

Our pilgrim life has been demanding, even arduous at times. So many things seemed—and sometimes were—a matter of life and death. Childhood illnesses gave way to middle school heartaches, which led inexorably toward adolescent growing pains so difficult I was forced to accept that we might not all make it out alive. If that sounds like hyperbole, I assure you it is not. From my writing desk, I sense many parents of struggling adolescents nodding their heads in agreement. It is difficult to grow up. It is difficult to grow up ourselves even as adults, and parenting has formed me like nothing else. There have been joyous freewheeling days when we were like clay in the potter's hand. There were nights when the fire of the kiln burned so intensely we wept and were tempted to despair.

The purpose of our placemaking shifted with the seasons and with the growth of our children. In the early days, we opened the many doors here at Maplehurst with abandon. Front door, back door, garden-side kitchen door, barn-side kitchen door—we flung them all open and hosted other people constantly, sometimes strangers, sometimes friends. When families came, we tossed our children in together and watched how quickly they learned to play hide-and-seek on all three floors of the house or flashlight tag across acres. Later, with the pandemic and teenagers, we learned how to open our doors with care. The black-painted barn we had built with dreams of a family reunion became a schoolroom for virtual learning. We began to understand that this house was not ours only but was home and haven for our children too. We moved our oldest up to the former guest room on the third floor. We gave each of our sons a room of his own. We accepted that Maplehurst could be a spacious place for us as well as for our guests. I learned that hospitality comes in many forms. We offer it to strangers, and we offer it to our own kids.

While pilgrims of old may have valued a staff, a hat, stout shoes, and a good canteen for water, we have needed tables and chairs for gathering, a sofa for naps, a garden for beauty, and trees for children to climb. We have needed desks for working, bedrooms for retreating, and a firepit around which we could make s'mores. We may carry more things than a typical pilgrim, yet truthfully these things have often carried us. Growing a marriage, raising children, loving our neighbors, serving our communities: such work is a privilege. It is full of purpose, but it is exhausting too. Sometimes a comfortable mattress and a bedroom blackout shade can make all the difference in the world.

To be a pilgrim is to walk through life motivated by a clear purpose and an aim. But there are

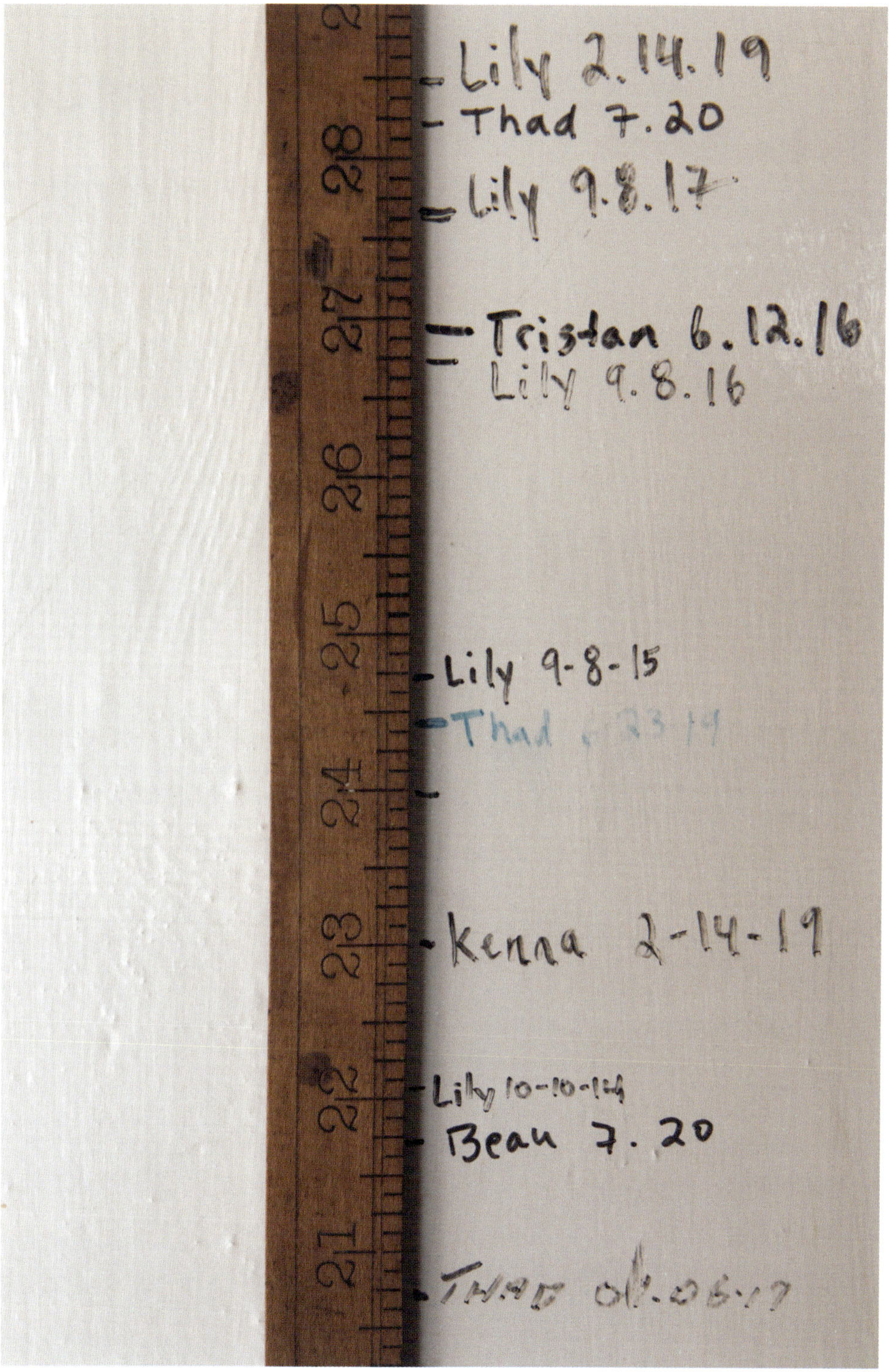

Lily 2.14.19
Thad 7.20
Lily 9.8.17
Tristan 6.12.16
Lily 9.8.16
Lily 9-8-15
Thad
Kenna 2-14-19
Lily 10-10-14
Beau 7.20
THAD

seasons when the purpose that seemed so clear can feel more like water slipping through our fingers. The aim that was sharp in our minds for so long is sometimes obscured by fog. Here at Maplehurst, I have learned that it is okay to release my grip on my dreams for a while. If certain dreams have been planted in me by God, then they do not need me to muscle them into reality: I can release them, I can open my hands. But whether we are aware of it or not, the dreams we release will often hold on to us. Sometimes we are only waiting for the thing we are sure has gone forever. When the fog finally clears, we may see ahead of us the dream we dropped miles back.

Maplehurst has fertile soil, perhaps from the Guernsey cattle once kept here, and this soil has shown me that dreams are cultivated like gardens. First, there is the smallest seed. It might manifest itself as you thumb through a magazine by the pool where your children swim, when you turn a page and feel your breath catch at the sight of a real estate ad for a large white farmhouse. Behind the house in the picture are enormous maple trees in full autumn glory. On the porch are four pumpkins. The house has a tall round tower, and you can suddenly see yourself writing in that tower room while four children play far below on the lawn. Except you are not a writer, and you only have three children, and you struggle with infertility, and you live in Florida where houses are one story and overhung with palm trees. And so as quickly as the dream blazes up like a flame, it dies back down. It is only a seed, but it has died in you, it has broken open in you, and things will never be the same.

Seeds are so small we can forget we carry them. In the daily work of tending our gardens, we can forget how it all began, how the soil was so bare and the emptiness seemed so absolute. Our winter waiting can feel endless when every circumstance of life seems to hold us back from doing anything at all to realize our dream. But then spring rises up like an open door, and that door leads to a dream come true, a promised land. Yet no sooner have you arrived than you are overwhelmed by tasks, by clearing and building and beginning, and so you hardly think of dreams. Until, one day, you are sitting up in the third-floor attic room that has become your office, with its two small windows and sloping ceiling. You are typing away at a book when the sound of children laughing pulls you toward the window. As you lean down, you remember how God brought you home to Maplehurst, how God gave you another daughter, how your dream of home grew into such an abundant garden it sometimes felt as if you might be buried under vines and leaves. And here you are, not buried but very much alive, and beginning to think of next year's garden. Your own children no longer play on the lawn down below, but the voices you hear of neighboring children sound like new dreams. You let yourself imagine a grandchild running across the lawn. You let yourself imagine a good and fruitful future.

Comforts for the Journey

This is not a shopping list. It is simply a recitation of some of the ordinary things that have brought me comfort at home along the way. What's on your list of home comforts? Let us give thanks for them together.

- First thing in the morning, I step into my bathroom, where an enormous seashell I found on an isolated beach in Alaska holds a bar of soap.
- The rising sun is already throwing rainbows across the tiled floor because we applied film in a clear etched-glass pattern to the lower panes of the bathroom window.
- An old wooden stool sits near my bedroom window. In summer, it holds a table fan. In winter, it holds a potted plant. This winter, it is a Swedish ivy with lavender flowers.
- When I walk downstairs in the morning, I pause to open the heavy lined curtains that cover a tall window at the curve of the stairs. The brass rings click and clack in a satisfying, old-fashioned way.
- At the bottom of the stairs, I pull back the curtains that cover our glass-paned front door. Even if the door were solid wood, we'd keep these green velvet curtains here because they shut out the winter drafts so well.
- I make my morning coffee in a glass pour-over carafe set into an olive wood stand. The bottom of the stand is now stained dark by years of coffee spills.
- I always wear slippers in the house. With wooden or tiled floors, they are a must, or I would drive myself crazy noticing crumbs.

- I keep a small table lamp on a tray on the kitchen counter. Lamplight is just right in the morning when making breakfast or in the evening when washing dishes.
- On the tray with the lamp are Harney & Sons tea tins. I keep them long after the tea is gone.
- Comfort is less critical during the bright middle of the working day, though I do keep a cushion on the seat of my desk chair and a warm shawl across the back. Comfort means the most on the tired edges, morning and evening.
- On cold evenings, I turn on the electric blanket and read in bed. On warm nights, I sit in the garden. Regular use of BTI granules in standing water helps keep the mosquito population low.
- I've been searching for the ideal temperature-regulating bedding for years now. For a while I thought I'd found it with linen, but even high-quality linen sheets seem to wear out quickly. Now I think I may have found it in bamboo. My summer sheets are bamboo fibers, and my favorite pajamas are too. I save the linen for winter, as it feels so warm to the touch but doesn't smother me at night like flannel.

Good night, Maplehurst. And thank you.

This Is the Day

I am a dreamer who is prone to nostalgia, which means I spend way too much of my time looking ahead and looking behind. This is a tragedy because the only place of encounter with God and with our neighbor is the present moment. This is the ordinary *right now*, pregnant with possibility, that the poet W.H. Auden called "the Time Being."[2] Always and again, I must remind myself that the best stories grow in the soil of our ordinary lives. It's where the magic happens. It's where goodness grows. It's nice to remember the lovely cup of coffee I enjoyed this morning, and it's sweet to anticipate the one I'll sip tomorrow. But everyone knows that the very best cup of coffee is the one I am slowly savoring exactly right now. The one right here in my hands.

When we still lived in Florida, toward the end of our difficult time there, I woke early one morning in the dark with these words floating through my mind: "This is the day that the Lord has made. Let us rejoice and be glad in it." I reached my hand to the other side of the bed before I remembered that Jonathan was traveling for work. Later that day he called me after leaving a meeting with his boss. "They've offered me a new job," he said, with a nervous smile I could hear over the phone. "It's time to look for a home." And I remembered the words from Scripture that had greeted me first thing in the morning. *This is the day. Let us be glad.*

Maplehurst in Pennsylvania has been a home of gladness. We have known loss here, and we have known deep pain, but the ordinary days with their ordinary comforts tell the story of these years best. I think of those words from the prophet Isaiah: "Every valley shall be lifted up, and every mountain and hill be made low... And the glory of the Lord shall be revealed" (40:4-5). Despite the highs and the lows of our own mountains and valleys,

Always and again, I must remind myself that the best stories grow in the soil of our ordinary lives. It's where the magic happens. It's where goodness grows.

I have felt the ground grow level beneath our feet as we have walked through life here. We have watched summer thunderstorms from the shelter of the front porch. We have laughed at groundhogs munching fallen apples from our kitchen windows. We have learned how to make good coffee here. Jonathan has finally perfected his pizza dough. We have picked wineberries on the wooded edges of the land. These berries are non-native and invasive, but they seem to grow even in the shade, and they look like jewels. If the world were any less wonderful, I'd be trying and failing to grow them in a garden bed. We have watched so many sunrises over the Black Barn and seen so many sunsets slip behind the garden shed. How many bedtime books have I read? How many breakfast pancakes has Jonathan flipped? How many fires have we stoked in the woodstove that warms our kitchen? Too many to count, and let us rejoice at that. God has been good to us in this place.

This house has proved itself to be the spacious place I first suspected it could be. It is spacious enough to hold yesterday, today, and tomorrow. It has held sorrow and joy and ordinary contentment. I am especially grateful for this quality because I am a visual person who lives in a visual culture that celebrates the beautiful moment: the flowers in bloom, the autumn woods at peak color, the perfectly plated restaurant meal just before we dig in our fork. We share visual highlight reels of our lives on social media, we love astonishing before-and-afters, and even our cooking websites give us photographs of colorful ingredients but never the dirty dishes. Is it any wonder I sometimes struggle to experience the goodness of the daily life I live in a place that needs continual care and attention? I love to feel immersed in beauty, but sunset is brief and the crumbs on my kitchen counter are almost endless. Yet I continue to find meaning in the tedium of caring for this house and this place. I know that the beauty we have made here is not as ephemeral as it can seem to be. Maplehurst is a house for all time, a shelter for us and for others whether we are young or old, sorrowing or rejoicing, or living out some quiet season of in-between.

It was gardening here at Maplehurst that first taught me to pay attention to the intersection of time and place. I kept trying and failing to create a pretty picture that would stay the same. I was trying to grow beauty that would resist decay, but that is neither a possible nor a worthy goal. In the garden, as everywhere in the earth, death and decay feed the seeds of new life. We make beauty by entering that cycle, not by fighting it. That truth has been harder to accept inside the house, but our homes and our lives and our world all grow along an arc of order, disorder, reorder. That is the true circle of life. When I repair or restore some part of Maplehurst, I want that repair to hold fast forever. I wish that newly painted walls would never grow dingy again, but when they do, it is an invitation to dream again, to be creative again. When the new baby born so soon after our arrival in this house turned six months old, a part of me really did want to keep her frozen in that moment when I could hold her completely and easily in my arms. But then I never would have heard her play a Christmas carol on the clarinet, or helped her rearrange the furniture in her room for a sleepover, or watched her pack away stuffed animals to make more room for art supplies. It is the swift growth of my four children that is teaching me how making a place sometimes involves seasons of unmaking. I am learning that letting go is as important as holding on.

While this house has changed a great deal in twelve years, the most astonishing changes are in the children themselves. Two have flown the nest for university. The baby is now nearly a teenager. The little boy who cried for his lost pajamas is learning to drive. Yet my husband and I do not feel changed. A little achier perhaps, but essentially we feel the same, and yet all around us are

IN GREEN

new people. These children are every day becoming themselves, and we are struggling to keep up, but there is joy in it, too, especially now that we understand how little is ours to control. We try to shape them, but they are also shaping us. Perhaps, after all, we are not the same either. When the son who sleeps in the bedroom next to ours seems to grow an inch in the night, I must anchor myself even more strongly in the present moment or I risk losing my balance in life altogether. I will waste too much time crying over years spent, lose myself in worries for their future, if I do not put down my phone, plant my feet, and get on with my day. Thankfully, Maplehurst helps me keep a rhythm to each day that is stabilizing and nourishing. Maplehurst has taught me that you can accomplish quite a bit from a posture of absolute trust and rest.

Here in this house, we have comfortable chairs for sitting, and I sit in them. In the morning, I drink my coffee in the pink armchair by the dining room's bay window. This is my corner for morning prayer. I have a candle and matches. I have a stack of wisdom books. There is my favorite icon of the face of Christ. His sorrowful eyes appear to have seen so much. This icon is a tangible reminder that God beholds us, and that is the greatest comfort I know. Here in this house and near the dining room, we have an old, slightly run-down kitchen in which my husband daily cooks breakfast for us. Scrambled eggs from our chickens (salt them, then let them sit for fifteen minutes for the best flavor, he reminds me), sour cream pancakes (a little extra protein, he says), and avocado toast (don't forget the bagel seasoning, I tell him). From my pink chair, I can hear him greeting our youngest. I can hear him asking if her brother is awake.

The wood frame of this chair is marked by dings and scratches. This is the favorite napping place of our cat Toby. He makes a beeline for it when we let him inside, which means the pink upholstery is usually dressed with a fair bit of black cat hair, as am I when I stand up again. But I don't love this chair because it is perfectly stylish or always immaculately clean. I love it because I know where to go first thing in the morning once I've made my cup of coffee. And knowing where to go next is sometimes half the battle. It is easy to be caught up in what our houses look like. We forget that houses matter because they give us places to sit, places to sip, places to eat, and places where we check in with one another. Home is where we begin each new day. Here in this house, I give thanks for this new day. The Lord made it. The Lord gave it. And right here, right now, in my pink chair, I rejoice in it.

Traditions

The Sacred Home

In his wonderful poem "How to Be a Poet," Wendell Berry reminds us that all places are sacred unless we actively desecrate them.[3] *While our homes—even at their messiest—have a kind of holiness because they are set apart, we can still tend them in ways that help feed our spiritual practices. The places we make can usher us toward the lives we want to live. That same poem opens with the simple yet astonishingly wise advice to make a place for sitting. And then sit, quietly, in the place we have made.*

- Designate a particular chair for prayer and keep a stack of inspiring books, like prayer books, devotionals, or Bibles, on a table nearby. In one of my favorite novels, Elizabeth Goudge describes what can happen when we devote ourselves to prayer in one particular place:

> *"Increasingly, as the years went by, her beautiful bedroom had become for her a sort of sanctuary. There was a deep peace in it... For so many years it was here that she had prayed most deeply and most often, so often, that now when she opened her bedroom door prayer brimmed up in her as automatically as it did when she crossed the threshold of...church."*[4]

- Keep a family prayer book, Bible, or gratitude journal on the table where you share your meals.
- Begin a collection of picture books or devotional books for seasons like Advent/Christmas and Lent/Easter.

- Keep faith-related picture books in a basket in the main family room; trade them out according to the season.
- Care for your home the way the altar guild cares for a church: fresh flowers, fresh linens, and good candles.
- Nurture family traditions that honor the story of your faith; for instance, we always take time on Epiphany (January 6) for a house blessing.
- Surround yourself with art that is meaningful to your faith.
- Adopt a simple litany for lighting a candle at the family dinner table; at Christmas, our candlelighter says, "Jesus Christ is the light of the world," and everyone at the table responds, "The light no darkness can overcome."

Center of Gravity

Some houses are so solid and enduring that they have a gravitational pull. They seem to draw objects toward themselves, and they hold the detritus of our daily lives in a tight embrace. They do not easily release anything, and the result is a basement where you might find a young boy's formal black bowler hat on a shelf near a wall-mounted pencil sharpener engraved with the year 1948. The attic of a house like this holds a stack of superfluous slate roof tiles 140 years after the workmen who laid the first roof placed them there for future repairs. Maplehurst is this sort of home, and so it is no wonder that gradually many beloved family heirlooms and familiar items of our childhoods, and many other things treasured enough but not quite enough, have passed from hand to hand and into our own hands here in Pennsylvania.

One of the first semiprecious pieces pulled into the orbit of this house was a curvy wooden wardrobe that once belonged to Jonathan's grandmother in Monterrey, Mexico. With a label inside proudly indicating that this wardrobe was made in England, it has a beautiful inset mirror, two rows of brass hooks, and rails with the kind of warm patina that needs many years to bloom. I can almost see the fur stoles and party dresses that must once have hung here. The wardrobe is exactly the right size to sit between the two built-in bookshelves at one end of our dining room. Jonathan's mother treasured the wardrobe but had no room for it in her own home. This story or one like it has been told to us again and again as we have welcomed a small armless rocking chair intended for sewing, a porcelain oil lamp painted in moody greens and mustard yellow, a tea set Jonathan's great-grandparents received as a gift when they wed more than a hundred years ago, an oval hall table, and a teetering pile of doilies crocheted by my own

I am also keenly aware that if every home refuses to receive the objects of our past, then future generations will have no access to Narnia. For where else do beautiful old wardrobes with glossy tiger-striped wood lead but to lands of enchantment? No particleboard shelving unit can take you there.

great-grandmother. Even the barn has received its share. On one knotty pine wall now hangs a large painting of a vase filled with pink roses that I remember loving when it hung on the wall of my grandmother's small Texas farmhouse.

Those who prefer a minimalist style of living might already find themselves shuddering. Even those who love antiques might be concerned about the line between homemaking and hoarding. That is a line I also consider, and I am learning that too many things in the home easily leads to the kind of disorder that feels like a burden, not a blessing. And yet I am also keenly aware that if every home refuses to receive the objects of our past, then future generations will have no access to Narnia. For where else do beautiful old wardrobes with glossy tiger-striped wood lead but to lands of enchantment? No particleboard shelving unit can take you there.

The abundance that turns a house into a home inheres in objects. To say this is not to give material objects more worth than they deserve—it is simply an observation of how our lives on this earth actually work. I wear a ring as a sign and symbol of my marriage. If I lose the ring, my marriage will be unchanged, but that is no reason not to treasure the ring my husband placed on my finger so many years ago. We belong to the present moment, but material things help connect us to the lives lived before ours and the lives that will come after. What connection would I feel to Jonathan's great-grandparents if not for the tea set that sits in my china cupboard? My thoughts would never go to them if not for a gold-rimmed ivory teapot painted with purple violets. Things can tell a story sometimes even better than words, and so many of the objects that have settled in this house turn ordinary moments into chapters in some long and still unfolding story.

THE ENCYCLOPEDIA OF Roses
DECORATING EDEN
THE ULTIMATE ROSE BOOK
PETER MCHOY
GARDENING ESSENTIALS
The Rose
AMERICAN ROSE SOCIETY
DARKE & TALLAMY
THE LIVING LANDSCAPE
THE GARDENS of COLONIAL WILLIAMSBURG
P. Allen Smith's GARDEN HOME
CREATING A FAMILY GARDEN
The Story of Flowers
Scots Roses
The COUNTRY Garden
The LAYERED GARDEN
THE INTIMATE GARDEN
What Makes a Garden
THE NEW GARDENER
GREENWOOD
A TREE IN THE HOUSE · HICKSON
COUNTRY GARDENS
Passion for Roses
ADVENTURES IN EDEN
THE ART OF GARDENING
Visions of Paradise
FLOWER HUNTER
Outstanding American Gardens
WINTERTHUR IN BLOOM
THE ELEGANT & EDIBLE G
NEW NATURALISM
Your Natural
SPIRIT OF
MODERN CONTAINER
Brilliant & Wild
DIRR'S ENCYCLOPEDIA
TREES & SHRU
BUNNY WILLIAMS
BRITISH and AMERICAN GARDENS
IN THE EIGHTEENTH CENTURY
The Well-Gardened MIND
KIMMERER BRAIDING SWEETGRASS
Old Roses and English Roses
MARC HAMER
Seed to Dust
A Proper Garden
The Problem with My Garden
A WEEKEND GARDEN GUIDE
CONTAINERS IN THE GARDEN
DALBY
Hybrid
DAFFODILS FOR AMERICAN GARDENS
Elizabeth and Her German Garden
BEHOLDING AND BECOMING
the BackYard Orchardist
Keeping Chickens with Ashley English
free-range chicken gardens
JESSI BLOOM
THE ILLUSTRATED BOOK OF TREES
KITCHEN GARDEN REVIVAL
GARDENING
Backyard Bouquets
THE NORTHEAST Native Plant Primer
ORCHARD HOUSE
1001 PLANTS TO DREAM OF GROWING
LIZ DOBBS
NOAH'S GARDEN
Fine Food, Wine and Pickled Pine
Keller
THE GARDEN in EVERY SENSE and SEASON
THRUSH GREEN
MISS READ
CHASING THE ROSE
OUDOLF HUMMELO
Better Homes and Gardens

Thrifting

Ordinary Heirlooms

Some heirlooms come from family and some come in a dusty cardboard box on the bottom shelf of the Salvation Army thrift store. Thanks to the many families who have let go of Grandmother's china, I have stocked our guest barn with thrifted china in a wild mixture of patterns. Most of it is not "fine" china, but even if it were, I would still wash it in the dishwasher. Call me silly or call me simple, but one of the great joys of my life is serving food to a large crowd and using no paper plates, no plastic cups, and no disposable flatware. If "wins" can sometimes feel hard to come by in life, this one is actually not that hard to achieve. It makes more sense financially (have you priced plastic cups recently?), it encourages the party to continue when the last guests join in to wash dishes, and everything can be stored in bins in the basement or in the drawers of a pretty pine dresser.

Here are some of the "heirlooms" I have found worth keeping and seeking out:

- Heavy brass candlesticks for the mantelpiece and table
- Silver-plated jugs and pitchers for flowers
- Small china saucers for keeping rings by the sink or jewelry on a dresser
- Real crystal glassware
- Sterling silver picture frames (even casual snapshots look amazing in silver)
- Punch bowls and punch cups for memorable parties
- Cloth napkins and tablecloths for everyday use and for special days

Grandfather Clock Time

As a child I was the proud owner of a seven-inch-tall grandfather clock, which may be why I have always felt there was a grandfather-clock-shaped hole in my home. Such a thing would never be practical in a third-floor Chicago apartment, and didn't feel right for our light and airy Florida ranch house either, but I knew Maplehurst deserved a stately timepiece from the moment I first walked inside. Seven inches in a dollhouse equals seven feet in a farmhouse, which sounds manageable, but only because a dollhouse clock has no heavy brass weights. A few years ago, I found a pristine grandfather clock for sale on Facebook Marketplace. I had been looking for a long while, but I didn't want to pay very much, and I didn't want to drive very far to pick it up. My idea had been to give this clock to my husband for Christmas. Few things justify buying a gift for yourself so well as wrapping it up for your spouse. I imagined myself slipping it into the back of our minivan and, well, the next step I hadn't thought through. Would I hide it under our bed? Would I store it at a friend's house? Would I keep it in our older son's bedroom? When the time came to pick up the clock I had agreed to buy, I did the only possible thing and confessed all to my husband: "I wanted to buy you a clock for Christmas! But I need your help loading it, and I can't figure out how to hide it."

THE STORY OF KENNETT
PEACOCK & VINE
A.S. BYATT
Barnwell
FOSTER
CLAIRE KEEGAN
SO LATE IN THE DAY
THE HIGH HILLS
JILL BARKLEM
WILLIAM MORRIS
BLACK NARCISSUS
RUMER GODDEN
METROPOLITAN
SEMINARS
PORTFOLIO 5 - COMPOSITION AS PATTERN

The actual clock was much bigger than the clock in my head. It would not fit into our minivan, would never have fit under our bed, and actually required my husband and another man to load it into the back of our pickup truck, while I carried the brass weights one by one because they were so heavy. But as soon as this grand old clock was in our home and chiming away every fifteen minutes, it seemed as if our household relationship to time shifted. Cellphone time races ahead, entirely linear, always moving, never arriving. But grandfather clock time moves *and* arrives—small arrivals every quarter hour and homecomings every hour on the hour. "I hear it! I hear it!" my younger son kept calling to me that first afternoon. "Can you hear the music? It must be four o'clock!" The present moment is a miracle worth noting and celebrating, because if we are honest with ourselves, the present moment is all we really have. The rest is memory and dream.

Most modern people have an anxious relationship with time. Time is the vessel they must fill—not only fill, but fill *well,* which we usually take to mean fill with as much as possible. It's like we're always engaged in a three-dimensional puzzle of sorts: how can I maximize? How can I be in two places at once? How can I squeeze as much productivity and efficiency out of every second, minute, and hour of my day? In my mind, I picture a jar filled with jelly beans. Ideally, those beans have as little "empty" space in amongst them as possible. Try to include other things in the jar, and suddenly many gaps open up. The most efficient way to fill that jar is with one thing only. Attempt to live a varied human life, and it can feel as if time is simply not cooperating. Ultimately, living as a placemaker has reformed my relationship to time. Now I know and accept that there is nothing efficient about beauty. There is nothing productive—at least in the usual sense—about curling up with a cable-knit throw on the purple sofa to watch flames dance in the old stone hearth. But that is what a well-kept home invites us to do. It asks that we stop moving and simply be. "Be still, and know that I am God," we read in Psalm 46 (verse 10). I like to think that God is always using this home I have made to draw me back toward the quiet stillness where he can be found.

When I was a child, I adored the book *Cheaper by the Dozen,* a hilarious semi-autobiographical novel based on the family life of renowned efficiency experts Frank and Lillian Gilbreth and their many children. The father brings his expertise in efficiency to the daily life of his large family with hilarious results, proving over and over that humans are not machines though they have marvelous minds and can make machines very well. Efficiency is not all wrong—after all, an efficient kitchen design really can make cooking easier

I like to think that God is always using this home I have made to draw me back toward the quiet stillness where he can be found.

and more enjoyable—but efficiency must not become an end in itself. Too much of what makes us human is profoundly inefficient. In her book on reimagining productivity, Jen Pollock Michel offers this profound insight on the relationship between time and place: "My hunch is that, in the absence of geographical stability, *time* has been substituted for *place* as the dominant context of modern life… We don't recognize we're rootless now, only that we are pressed for time."[5] I am aware that my life offers a kind of proof for Michel's hunch. The daily practice of rooting myself in this home has somehow filled my life with what I can only call timeless moments.

Places—and especially our own homes—help us step out of *chronos* (or clock time) and into *kairos* (or meaning-full time). In *Four Quartets,* the poet T.S. Eliot describes an ultimate *kairos* moment as a kind of stillness at the center of the world. This is the place, he says, where past and future converge.[6] Maplehurst is the still point of my world. By living a life rooted in place (even if we must occasionally pick up our roots and move to some other place), we are enabled to live lives full of meaning apart from how we *use* our time. Meaning is no longer correlated only with movement. We will still *do* the work of living, but we will also stop and listen to the music of the moment. We will be able to hear the song of *Right Now.* It's a song that can sound like many things. Here at Maplehurst, it sounds like the Westminster chime melody.

Keeping Time

Life is change, because life is growth. But in the midst of constant change, traditions offer moments of return. With every tradition kept, we can say, "Here we are again. The same but new." Traditions are a predictable comfort in anxious, uncertain times.

Here are a few of our favorite Maplehurst traditions (some we still keep, some we keep only in our memories):

- Cutting down a real tree at the local Christmas tree farm (they are never the prettiest or most stylish, but they are uniquely ours)
- Watching our neighbor's fireworks show every Fourth of July (not the fanciest, but we have front-row seats)
- Leaving our Halloween candy outside our bedroom doors so that the "Candy Fairy" can exchange all of the candy children with food allergies can't eat with a new toy or other gift
- Eating pizza on Friday nights (from freezer pizzas early in our marriage to fresh from the wood-fired oven now)
- Staying home on New Year's Eve and serving up sushi (because our children love it, but it costs a fortune)
- Lighting candles at the dinner table every night after we turn the clocks back

- Baking my Thanksgiving stuffing in a Bundt pan to give it a pretty shape before turning it out onto a cake stand
- Arranging homegrown flowers on store-bought summer birthday cakes
- Picking strawberries in June at the local farm and eating strawberry shortcake for dinner
- Going on Easter egg hunts with the neighbors
- Hiding our Christmas Nativity set somewhere in the garden on Christmas Day (when the sun sets, we go in search of baby Jesus, guided by votive candles—after we find him, we sing "Silent Night")
- Making a "King Trifle" instead of a "King Cake" for Epiphany (trifles are quicker and easier to put together than cakes—and whoever finds the baby Jesus charm doesn't have to help with dishes!)
- Dressing up for Christmas Day dinner (if Mom and Dad go to the trouble to make a feast, the children can at least change out of their pajamas, and a festive dinner at the end of the day helps the whole day feel special)
- Lighting a bonfire on the shortest day of the year
- Making flower crowns on the longest day of the year

A Sofa for the Kitchen

A Victorian sofa with a frame of curvy carved wood rests against one wall of our kitchen here at Maplehurst. The sofa has a story, as vintage finds often do, but until I sat down to write about it, I hadn't realized how far back this story goes. I first saw the sofa in a Florida thrift shop on a day when I was desperately sick with winter allergies and desperately heartsick for a new farmhouse home, one located where the skies dropped snowflakes in winter and not tree pollen. I saw the old-fashioned curves of this couch and thought, *That is the right sofa for a farmhouse.* In a rash act of optimism and hope, I bought the sofa, drove back to my seashell-stuccoed ranch house, told my husband I had something he needed to pick up, and then promptly cleared space in our garage for the future. While I prayed for a new job for my husband and a new home for our family, I put faith into action and called an upholsterer whose name I found online. I bought a length of ivory trim and yards of indoor-outdoor fabric in a pale green herringbone pattern. Then I waved goodbye to my sofa as the upholsterer hauled it away in his van. It would be a long while before we were reunited.

The first two kitchens of our married life were tiny apartment-sized galley kitchens hardly large enough for Jonathan and me to stand side by side. Our third kitchen in a modest Virginia townhouse was a giant by comparison and spacious enough to hold a table by the bay window. "An eat-in kitchen!" our real estate agent exclaimed when we first stepped inside. Having just graduated from college, we owned only one small table, so we chose to place our pride and joy—an antique oak pedestal table with a single crack

in the base—in the corner of the living room we called "the dining room." We felt it earned that name because of a pass-through window from the kitchen, though we never passed dishes that way. When we bought new matching love seats for the living room in a very impractical but very beautiful white, we tucked our old love seat into the kitchen's bay window. Jonathan had bought that sofa himself from an elderly neighbor in Texas, knowing he would soon move out of his college dorm, marry me, and move into a shared apartment. Thanks to his foresight, we had a spare sofa, and my love affair with kitchen sofas had officially begun.

Because we left Texas and Virginia for life in Chicago's South Side, it would be many, many years before we lived in a house with a room large enough for another kitchen sofa. I'm not sure a lot of people would have looked at the kitchen here at Maplehurst and thought it roomy enough for a couch, but we tucked a spare love seat along the wall near that same oak pedestal table the day we moved in. Instead of two, we were now five, and we soon added a baby in a high chair. But we

If you think about it carefully,
every sofa can be a love seat.

spend so much time in our kitchens, so why not be comfortable? As a parent, I've learned that a sofa with a throw blanket and a few pillows has the power to keep a child or even a teenager close by while I cook, something that a stool at the island or a chair at the table just can't do. If you do not want company while you read a recipe, do not put a sofa in your kitchen. Of course, I have even been known to stretch out with a novel while waiting for my oven timer to beep.

In Florida, weeks turned into months, and we had no news of a job and no word from the upholstery shop. That June, my thirty-fifth birthday came and nearly went, but toward the end of the day, the phone rang. A voice in my ear said, "I'm sorry for the last-minute call, but I'm in your neighborhood. Your sofa is finished. Can I bring it by?" And that is how I received a farmhouse sofa for my thirty-fifth birthday. Later, it seemed as if the sofa—which may have been an impulse buy or may have been an act of faith (or could it have been both?)—was the thing that nudged us finally over the crest of some invisible hill and down, in a rush, toward our future. Two days after my birthday, Jonathan received a job offer. One week later, Jonathan and I were flying to Philadelphia to look for a new home near his new job. Three weeks after that, we were moving into Maplehurst, where my thrifted Victorian sofa looked right at home in the Victorian front parlor and our old one fit perfectly along the kitchen wall. A few years ago, we put a new purple sofa in the parlor and shifted my birthday couch to the kitchen. When I tell friends you never know what treasure you might find in a thrift store, I mean it, because I've found it. And if you think about it carefully, every sofa can be a love seat.

FRENCH COUNTRY COOKING

Thrifting

Always Thrift, Sometimes Thrift, Rarely Thrift

ALWAYS

There are certain things I simply do not allow myself to buy new. This may be because new is so expensive (dishes) or maybe because new is less well-made (wooden furniture). Or it may simply be that there is so much available on the secondhand market that it makes little sense to buy new (flower vases). Here is what I always buy secondhand:

- Lamps (new ones are often expensive and poorly made)
- Wooden furniture like tables, dressers, desks, chairs
- Rugs (vintage, hand-knotted rugs can easily be found for the price of new machine-made synthetic rugs)
- Dishes, fancy and everyday
- Silverware and flatware
- Vases
- Candlesticks
- Garden ornaments and statuary

SOMETIMES

These are the items I sometimes buy new and sometimes thrift. It depends on whether I need a perfect piece (I bought a new leather sectional sofa because it fit the strange dimensions of our family room exactly) or can make room for something less than perfect.

- Upholstered furniture like sofas and armchairs
- Curtains
- Glassware (I love thrifting crystal but sometimes only a new, perfectly shaped wine glass will do)
- Outdoor furniture (I love buying teak furniture secondhand, but outdoor cushions I often buy new)
- Art (I look for old art at estate sales and auctions, but I also love choosing special pieces from local artists)

- Garden planters (new terra-cotta is inexpensive and versatile, but I like looking for heavy-duty concrete planters and terra-cotta pots with patina)
- Table linens
- Frames (thrifted frames are a great way to build a gallery wall, but quality framing from a local craftsperson is a worthwhile investment for special pieces)

RARELY

These items can be thrifted, but I tend to buy them new in order to update my thrifted pieces. A new shade on an old lamp can take it in an entirely new style direction. A fresh pillow for an antique sofa? It's a match made in heaven. And unless I'm looking for a vintage copper pot, I choose new, high-quality cookware (like enameled cast iron) that can last a lifetime.

- Lampshades (new shades can make a room instantly stylish)
- Cushions, accent pillows, throw blankets
- Bed linens
- Cookware and appliances

Beauty Invites

When we first moved to Maplehurst, the kitchen had been renovated by the previous owners about seven years before. I don't know how the room was heated prior to this renovation, or even whether it had been heated at all, but these particular owners added electric floor heating beneath new ceramic tiles. The rest of the house was heated with a radiator system powered by a boiler in the basement, but because the old kitchen would once have been warmed by a wood- or coal-fired cookstove, it has no radiators. Without those new underfloor coils, it had no heat. Our first autumn and winter at Maplehurst were quite cold, and we dialed up the thermostat for the kitchen floor. Our little kids loved to feel the warmth through their footed pajamas. Then our postal carrier dropped the first electric bill in the mailbox at the far end of our long driveway, and when we opened it, our jaws dropped in horror. We immediately turned the kitchen thermostat down and added a layer of clothing. That winter, the house was comfortable, but the kitchen was an actual icebox. The tiles were still warm, but we had learned that the amount of electricity they required in order to shift the temperature of the room was far too much.

I am an artist married to an engineer, which sounds like a problem but is actually (on most days) a match made in heaven. Too much sameness in a marriage can be a serious liability. For instance, Jonathan and I are both dreamers and visionaries who love to begin new projects but struggle to attend to the details of the many projects we have already begun. We partner best when my eye for beauty and his eye for construction gaze productively in the same direction. While I'm gathering wallpaper and paint samples, he runs off to the hardware store to check the width of the beadboard paneling and see what our options are for in-stock trim and molding. He likes to say that I dream it and he builds it. Thankfully, he says this with a smile. Jonathan approached the problem of our cold kitchen like an engineer and brought in an electric space heater and made plans to add insulation as soon as we could. My own answer to any house question is always the same: beauty. This is often enormously impractical and unhelpful, but when I'm right, I am gloriously right. Even Jonathan says so. If your primary love language is beauty and your kitchen is cold, where does your mind wander? Do you think of HVAC systems or portable units or new, more-efficient floor coils? You do not. You remember the cookstove that would once have been in this room, you scroll through images of Nordic dream houses, and you tell your husband that the solution is actually a woodstove. But not any woodstove! The kitchen is not enormous, after all, and we do still need room for the sofa. But look, right here, is the most beautiful woodstove in the world. "Is that a squirrel?" your husband asks, squinting at the image on your phone.

That is, indeed, a squirrel.

We've heated our kitchen with a Danish Morsø cast-iron woodstove for a decade now. It's a small black stove that fits right along one wall, leaving room for the birthday sofa on the other wall. This woodstove is so well built that, unlike many other stoves, it requires no electricity to power a fan. Because my asthma does not do well with open fires, watching the flames dance behind the stove's glass window is a special treat. I've heard it is possible to keep the glass squeaky-clean with newspaper dipped in damp wood ash, but I always forget to try this while the glass is cold and the stove unlit. As well, our Morsø includes the classic raised design on the sides of the stove: a squirrel encircled by oak leaves and acorns. This woodstove is more beautiful than it needs to be, which in my opinion is always the right answer, always the best solution, and the perfect marriage of poetry and prose.

Does the beauty that feeds our souls require sacrifice? That is one way to ask the question, but my answer uses different terms. I think that beauty invites our participation, and on very cold mornings, especially if Jonathan is out of town and my sons are sleeping in, I wish I could flick a switch for warmth. If we haven't stocked our woodpile outside the kitchen door, you will really hear me grumble as I search for kindling in my slippers. Sourcing firewood, storing firewood, chopping firewood, stacking firewood, collecting kindling, and learning to start a fire quick and hot and without smoke—these are the ways we participate in the care that beauty offers us. If it all sounds like too much sacrifice, I will mention as well that our neatly stacked woodpile now serves as a cozy and clever screen for our garbage cans. I stand by these words: beauty is always a good answer, even if budgets and marriages sometimes ask that we compromise. The woodstove in our Black Barn has no squirrel, but the flames are just as warm, just as beautiful. Call it sacrifice if you must. Call it the price of beauty. I prefer to think of it as joining in. Beauty involves us, and I am glad to be included.

Inspiration

Practical, Beautiful, or Both?

Few things please me more than finding beautiful solutions to practical needs. As I type this, I can see out of the corner of my eye a small porcelain vase I brought home from a charity shop in England (their version of our thrift stores). It's a Wedgewood piece in a wild strawberry pattern, but it isn't the most practical size or shape for flowers. What it is, however, is a perfectly beautiful storage solution: this one holds pens and pencils on my desk, and another similar vase holds makeup brushes in my bathroom.

Over the years, certain beautiful practicalities have become second-nature in our home. I take them for granted, which is as it should be for all children of a beautiful God. Beauty is our birthright.

- Keep dish soap and olive oil in glass bottles with pour tops.
- Decant maple syrup into a stoppered glass jug (makes warming in the microwave easier too).
- Learn a quick-and-easy vinaigrette recipe and ditch the ugly containers of store-bought (and less healthy) salad dressings on your table.
- Store cloth napkins in a basket on or near the kitchen table (toss some in regularly as you do laundry—no more need for paper napkins).
- Use clear glass or plastic food storage containers in the pantry (wide tops work best for baking ingredients like flour and sugar).
- Switch to bar soap in the bathroom, a more sustainable practice that requires less packaging (in your guest bathroom, create delicate single-serving slivers of soap with a vegetable peeler and arrange them on a dish when guests are due).
- Not enough closet space? Find a clothing rack on wheels and fill it with your prettiest pieces worthy of display.
- Need something pretty in an entryway or mudroom entrance? One of my college professors kept her collection of silk scarves on pegs near her front door—beautiful and convenient.

Let There Be Light

Like many older homes, Maplehurst was positioned with great care. In a sense, the house has two faces. The first is narrow with a pair of very tall parlor windows looking down the long driveway toward the street. This face looks north. The second front is wide and oriented toward the west. The front door is on this side, as is the beautiful bay window in our dining room. Long ago, carriages would pull right up to this door before heading on around the house toward the barn in the back. Rerouting the driveway so that it turns at the home's front porch gave us a proper backyard, but it means that no one sees the home's western front, its front door and its bay window, unless they choose to step into the garden.

The house is like a compass. The front parlor is north, the kitchen windows are brilliant, sunny south. The bay window catches the sunset. The window at the top of the stairs frames the moonrise in the east. The house is a vessel for light, catching it, holding it, filling some rooms with it while keeping others in dim, cool shadow. Because the color and intensity of the light varies so much from room to room here at Maplehurst, I have gained an intimate knowledge of the position of the sun in various seasons and how the different kinds of light make me feel. I do not keep potted plants near my kitchen windows in summer, because the sun is too high in the sky to touch them. In winter, I crowd the countertop with potted geraniums and hot peppers and watch as the low sun bathes them in light all day long. And I am not so different from a potted plant. I, too, follow the light in winter, the shade in summer. My small office on the third floor faces north and has only two small windows, though they are beautifully curved on top. It is a cool, quiet place to work in summer. But in winter, I prefer my own bedroom, which sits

I am not so different from a potted plant. I, too, follow the light in winter, the shade in summer.

on the second floor above the dining room. Here is a bay window facing west, a continuation of the window below. Here also is another large window facing south. I could spend a whole winter lying in bed and never grow tired of the warm light, the dancing shadows, the fire of the sunset as the day drops behind the trees.

Sometimes I long for a modern home with enormous glass windows and an open floor plan. What a gift it must be to live in a box filled with light. Other times I wish for an old-fashioned conservatory with more than enough room for every potted plant I grew in summer. But Maplehurst is my home, and I am grateful for its particular light. It is a compass, and it is a clock. It orients me as I climb the stairs and peer from the windows. It registers the minutes of the day beautifully as the sun shifts from window to window, from room to room. If we are building a house, we can and should consider the light. When my mother-in-law first moved to Pennsylvania to make her home with us, we chose the position of her cottage, and especially the large window that would fill the wall above her kitchen sink, by using one of my favorite gardening tools: an app called Sun Scout that shows the position of the sun on any given day of the year. She wanted to see the sunrise from that window in the morning, and now—if the clouds cooperate—she does.

But what if you live in a home like my Chicago apartment, where windows were few and far between? What if you live in a row house? A basement unit? A dark forest? Then it is even more important to watch and wait for the light. If the sun floods your living room for just a few minutes in the evening, then that is the spot for dinner parties and bedtime stories and the Christmas tree. Just as it is in winter, when we have less sunlight, it matters more. It means more. We learn not to squander the gift. I finally stopped squandering the gift of light in my own home when I disregarded the common advice to *never work in your bedroom* and moved a small desk to the end of my bed. Now on winter days when my dim office does not beckon, I move from bed to desk and back again like the sun gliding across the sky. Other people chose the position of this house with care. Now I am cared for in turn simply by noticing and receiving the light.

Living out of Control

Sometime during our second year at Maplehurst, Jonathan and I drove our pickup truck practically all the way to Philadelphia to buy a vintage rolltop desk I had found in an online listing. This desk wasn't just another piece of furniture. It was the key to my plan to regain control of our finances. I told myself that a desk like this one, in a spot convenient to the kitchen, not only would provide a practical and convenient place for tracking our budget and paying bills on our laptop computer, but would also allow for all of the paperwork to be neatly hidden beneath the accordion folds of the pull-down top. Surely, with a desk like this close at hand, I could keep an eye on our newly walking one-year-old while entering receipts into the spreadsheet Jonathan had made for us.

The desk's previous owners admitted they had lost the antique skeleton key that could lock and unlock the roll top itself. "When I find it, I'll mail it to you!" the young woman told me. I might have realized then that this desk would not be the key to regaining a sense of control over a life that was growing in unpredictable directions. I might have guessed we would pile so many things on this beautiful desk that we would only occasionally be able to pull down the wooden cover, let alone lock it. For years now, the chaos of its contents has generally spilled over, not with my laptop and orderly paperwork but with coloring books, craft paints, art pencils, and the many chargers, cords, and plugs that power family life these days. I have also kept one drawer stuffed with sheets of bubble wrap. My hope that I will recycle this wrap into other packages springs eternal, though I never think of this drawer or its contents until new bubble wrap enters

my life. I do occasionally attempt to organize the contents of this desk, throwing out the crustier paints and the coloring books that are mostly full, and I find peace in that work. But the desk is a constant reminder that, as dedicated placemakers and old-house caretakers, we have said first a tentative and now an enthusiastic yes to a life that is not ours to control.

I thought I would find peace in an orderly, predictable family budget. Instead, I have found peace by letting that ideal go. It began when we came home to Maplehurst in August. Early that September, our fourth child was born. In November, an oil truck from a local supplier pulled into our driveway. I can still see the driver hopping down from his seat behind the wheel and beginning to snake a long hose toward the western side of our house. He seemed to know exactly where he was going, but back then I was only vaguely aware of the oil-fueled boiler in our basement that would heat the water that would flow through our radiators that would warm the rooms of this house all winter. We'd moved from Florida and hadn't experienced a real winter in years. The combination of a new house with unforeseen old-house needs and a new baby with unforeseen new-baby needs was like a bomb going off in the midst of our careful family budget. We had always budgeted with precision, tracking every expense and every receipt, but now it seemed that we had no idea what our expenses would be. We suddenly found we needed baby formula. But how much? We needed heating oil. But, again, how much? We also needed snow removal. But how often? The budget we had carried with us from Florida quickly lay in proverbial tatters at our feet. My ability to forecast an accurate budget felt as reliable as the weather report.

It's all very well to go on about beauty and light and creating a house to call home, but are such concerns only for the very rich? Or, at least, the very comfortable? The ones with income to spare? That day, when the oil delivery man tied his first receipt to the knob of our front door, I sat in the baby's room, holding her in the white-painted rocking chair I'd carried from Chicago to Florida to Pennsylvania. Maybe it was my anxiety about the number I would see on that receipt, maybe it was the fault of those postpartum hormones, but I suddenly felt drenched with worry. It wasn't only the heating bill. It was a list of home repairs a mile long. It was a list of hoped-for home improvements another mile long. And somehow, rocking slowly in that chair, I also began to fret about the cost of four college educations. I had prayed desperate prayers through infertility for every one of my children. I had prayed and hoped and dreamed for two years in our Florida wilderness for this house. And now I was terrified by the responsibility for these many answered prayers. My inability to corral the numbers of our budget into the neat columns of the spreadsheet Jonathan had set up for us began to seem like a premonition of disaster. I felt sure that if this life and this house were a calamity in the making, I would have only myself to blame. Wasn't I the one who had longed for children, who had dreamed of an old farmhouse to call home? I'd made my bed, as the saying goes, and now I lay in that bed most nights awake with worry.

That day, still in the rocking chair, I began to read my Bible, and in the Old Testament I found a promise, not only for ancient people in a faraway place but for me, now, at Maplehurst, my farmhouse whose name means maple hill: "And I will make them and the places round about my hill a blessing; and I will send down the showers in their season; they shall be showers of blessing" (Ezekiel 34:26). I read those words and was comforted that winter. In the spring and summer, the rains began to fall, and by June we were breaking all-time records for rainfall in our corner of Pennsylvania. All that rain seemed to me like a seal on the promise that God would provide and God would bless, and we would "dwell securely" with our young at Maplehurst. And yet I never expected that provision could be so uncomfortable just as I never anticipated how all that rain would rot the squash and pumpkins growing in our first garden.

I began to notice a pattern of provision in those first few years of life in this house. First, some great need would arise. The house required air-conditioning if we were going to use the third floor for guests in summer or the windows needed repairing before the sills rotted clean away. I would hem and haw and fret and worry before finally I remembered to pray. Then some miracle of provision would drop like a falling star: a phone call alerting us to some old insurance policy we needed to cash in right now, or a sudden unexpected bonus arriving with that month's paycheck. But the provision—and here's the rub—would always be close but not quite enough. Always there was this gap, and we would stand on the edge wondering, *If we jump, will we fall? Or land safely on the other side?* I thought God would meet our needs like a gentle rain. Mostly, it has felt more like spluttering and trying to catch my breath while cold, sharp needles of rain drench me to the skin. *All right, Lord,* I have learned to say with laughter and with hope, *I'm soaking wet, and I'll probably slip and fall, but here I go with this running leap. Here I go with no safety net but you.*

OAT MEAL
IRISH OATME

BROTHER'S PIZZA

PART THREE

The Comforts of Community

"The first thing to happen in this house," she said softly, solemnly, "shall be a kiss."

ELIZABETH VON ARNIM,
THE ENCHANTED APRIL

The Work of Many Hands

We were ten years at Maplehurst before we felt that sense of fulfillment and completion that is the hope and aim of every dreamer. I had not realized it would take so long. I certainly did not expect that in the end it would not even be my idea that would lead us to the work that would feel so much like an arrival. Even artists who create in isolation require that generative seeds occasionally blow in on the wind, and I have never been an isolated artist, no matter how appealing that has sometimes seemed to me. Ultimately, the seed for our Maytime garden party was planted by my editor Ruth, who asked, "Will you host a party to celebrate the release of *Garden Maker*?" I tend to know that an idea is not only good but right when it feels something like a sticker bur, those clinging seeds that would catch a ride to new soil tangled on my socks and shoelaces when I was a child visiting my grandmother's farm in Texas. The idea of a garden party landed on me like a hooked seed I couldn't shake off.

How could I plan and execute something so ambitious while writing a follow-up garden book? And how could I even dream of hosting a crowd when our Black Barn was still home to my mother-in-law and not available as a party space? Eventually, my particular questions devolved into the general doubts I always feel before opening the door of my home: what if the weather is awful? What if no one comes, or they don't have a good time? What if the preparations cause too much stress in my life? What if I simply can't pull it off? And yet threaded through every doubt and every question was an emerging picture of neighbors wandering through the flower garden at golden hour with glasses in their hands and music in the air. I began to see them gathered around the wood-fired pizza oven, my husband's longtime dream fulfilled. I began to hear laughter and see candlelight and imagine everyone leaving with a new plant for their own garden. Though I was still unsure if I should do it, this garden party began to seem like a blank page on which I could already read the opening sentence of a wonderful story.

We have hosted many parties and gatherings over the years at Maplehurst. It was not immediately apparent to me that this one would be so different. Every time, it begins with a dream or an idea, a nudge or a desire. These must be strong enough to override most of my worries and objections, of which I always have many. Sometimes the vision is that strong, and the results have been as varied as a literary Twelfth Night dinner party, a flower-fairy tea party, and a Midsummer Eve spent chasing fireflies and making flower crowns.

On reflection, the garden party was different from the beginning. It was different because I knew with certainty I could not manage it on my own, and I asked an artistic friend to help me. I told myself that she would do most of the planning, and I would be free to continue work on my book. I imagined sailing into a garden party that someone else had created, but of course it was nothing like that. It is always good when we don't know how much effort will be required of us. I might never leave my bed if I knew, and I would certainly never plan a party, and yet I would miss

so much. In the end, my friend became very sick the day of the party and couldn't make it at all, but the questions she had asked me in the beginning—questions about a theme and a story for the evening, questions about what I envisioned—pushed me to imagine something better than I would have dreamed up on my own. My own imagination is always hampered by what I think is possible. When we imagine, we must let ourselves wander into the impossible, but I tend never to go there without a good push and some company along the way.

My artist friend introduced me to her own new friend, whose family owned a local winery whose specialty was a Spanish-style vermouth flavored with black walnuts just like the ones that drop onto the roof of our Black Barn each fall. With sparkling water and an orange slice, it made an instant garden cocktail. The winery family just happened to know a musician who sang jazz standards with a talented band. Before connecting with the jazz singer over the phone, I told my husband that I wished I could find something like an ice cream truck that would serve a dessert more elegant than ice cream. At the end of my call confirming the date with the singer, she casually mentioned that her husband—who hailed from France—had just created a food truck for serving authentic French dessert crepes. *If we might want something like that at our party?* When I told her that is exactly what I wanted at my party, I don't think she understood how much I meant what I said.

On and on it went, as if suddenly I was being shown how wide and deep our community had grown in the decade of our living here. For years, we had allowed the teachers at a nearby school to use our property for overflow parking. The administration immediately said yes when we asked if we could borrow the school's golf cart to help transport guests and their plant purchases down the length of our driveway. My husband had ordered pizza and tipped generously in cash and conversation at our local pizzeria for so many years that when he asked if anyone there knew how to make pizza in a wood-fired oven, the owner himself came to toss dough and wouldn't take a penny for his time or his toppings. When I asked my friend who owns her own native plant landscaping business if she might like to sell plants at the party, she asked if she could create custom, themed garden plant collections. And I may have been a bit teary when I responded in the affirmative. *Yes, please, that's even better.*

Asked as a child, I told the well-meaning adults in my life I wanted to be an artist when I grew up. One Halloween I even dressed as an artist with one of my father's shirts as an oversize smock, a red beret on my head, and a homemade paint palette in my hand, but what did that word *artist* mean to me at ten years old? It meant paints and pencils, though I was not exceptionally skilled with either. By using that word, I was responding to—without being able to name—the things I loved most: beauty and color, history and home. A few years later, that artistic urge would lead me to say I wanted to become an interior designer; still later, that I would be an architect. I never would have guessed writer and placemaker. I would not have understood that artists can make books and gardens and also garden parties. And I could not have known that some works of art require a whole community that has been cultivated over years.

That a party can be a work of art was an idea latent in me since childhood. Probably the idea first came to me through books. There was the sugaring-off dinner and dance at Grandpa's house in *Little House in the Big Woods* with its inspiring combination of seasonal necessity and enjoyment. I know I was influenced by Marilla's kitchen in *Anne of Green Gables*, though I was never quite sure I understood the critical difference between raspberry cordial and currant wine. There was the Christmas feast for the woodland animals so cruelly interrupted by the White Witch in Narnia.

Parties and feasts bring a place to life in the service of community and friendship. If Monday night supper is a quick pencil sketch, a garden party for eighty guests is an oil painting. Framed. In gold leaf. The creative desire that leads me to write or to plant a flower garden is also the spark that leads me to plan parties. I may be an introverted wallflower, but I love to envision something beautiful and then invite other people into it. And yet, whether I was recalling our annual neighborhood-wide Easter egg hunts or the barn blessing with barbecue or the Advent open house, I always felt a sense of aiming yet falling ever so slightly short. Some gatherings came quite close to feeling perfect, others seemed to me redeemable only as "learning experiences," but I almost always looked back on them all and wondered why my dreaming and planning left me feeling as if I could never quite realize a vision in full.

The early May garden party was different, and the difference was made up entirely of all the people who helped me create it. For ten years, we had been hosting at Maplehurst, but the kind of party I was always aiming for was the kind I could not make on my own. It needed a community of hosts, and that community needed time to grow. My ambition for a great gathering needed my French friend Stéphanie creating the most beautiful table of fruit-filled water in glass vessels alongside tiers of colorful French macarons. It needed my friend Elrena, who claims to have no domestic skills yet knew to provide the band with convenient glasses of water, something that had not occurred to me. It needed my friend Melissa, who not only hustled all day moving furniture and placing candles but was also willing to spend the entire party quietly sitting at the book and merchandise table

Flowers
Peonies
GARDEN MAKER
GARDEN MAKER

Parties and feasts bring a place to life in the service of community and friendship.

in the party tent selling my books and chatting with everyone who came to shop for garden plants. It needed my sons in matching bow ties escorting guests up and down our driveway in the golf cart. It needed friends who felt as if this house was their home too: friends like Lisa-Jo, Jen, and Allison. All of these friends welcomed the party guests as if Maplehurst was their very own home, because time spent in that place with us had made it theirs. They weren't merely helpers; they were hosts in their own right. The artful gathering I had always wanted, without knowing exactly what it was I desired, couldn't be achieved with a hired team (though there are certainly times when hiring a team is exactly the right call). It could only be the creation and offering of a community—the fruit of many years of friendship.

The artist friend who had helped me dream with more ambition and imagination also introduced me to a friend of hers who is a wedding and event photographer. The photographs she took that evening are works of art in their own right, and I printed and framed two favorites for our home. The first hangs in my bedroom. Framed in white, it is a dreamy image of the flower garden with its white garden shed, taken just as I stepped onto the garden path in my floaty pale-pink party dress. The second image hangs on our second-floor landing, and I think it looks like a vintage cinema poster for some wonderful old French art film. It shows a group of guests gathered at the window of the bright blue crepe truck. The crepe maker smiles from inside the vehicle, backlit in the darkness by the truck's interior lights. The sun sets behind the background trees, and the light shining through the black branches looks like a sky full of stars. In a puddle of light at the front of the truck is my young daughter in a strawberry-print dress, her arms spread wide. The photographer has caught her mid-twirl. She is not typically a dancer, but it was a night for twirling. It was a night for unexpected joy.

Thrifting

Furnishing a Garden

"Necessity is the mother of invention" may be an over-familiar proverb, but don't let that stop you from believing it. When we built a large concrete patio behind our house, complete with a beautiful central fire bowl, we needed large-scale furniture for gathering with friends and family around the fires we intended to build. But our house is large, which meant the patio was large, and in keeping with that scale, the fire bowl was also—you guessed it—large.

I quickly despaired of finding anything in the right scale at a price we could afford, but that didn't stop me from searching through every online resource I could find. My frustration grew as I realized that even the right-sized and very expensive pieces I liked would probably not last more than a few years. I felt sick at the thought of spending that much money for outdoor furniture that would eventually get tossed into some landfill. As has happened so often in my years of making a home, I was saved from a terrible mistake by a lack of money.

While scrolling Facebook Marketplace hoping someone might be ridding themselves of a patio set large enough for our space, I began to notice just how many people were offering old, rusty wrought iron garden furniture for sale. In styles and ages ranging from Victorian to art deco and mid-century modern, wrought iron has been a popular choice for patio furniture for many years. Before the contemporary proliferation of synthetic materials, wrought iron was one of the few substances that could take a beating from the

weather. Part of my dilemma had always come from imagining the kind of furniture that could fit with an old Victorian farmhouse and a newly built concrete patio. I liked the contrast of Victorian house and modern concrete, but should the furniture go one way, or the other? When I found an especially old and especially large wrought iron outdoor sofa, I found my answer. If I could gather up enough old pieces, I could paint them a single unifying (and modern!) color. Best of all, for the price of patio furniture from a big-box store, I could have furniture that would essentially last forever.

That winter, I began collecting wrought iron garden furniture in all different patterns and styles. I could have cleaned them and spray-painted them myself, but I wanted a durable finish and didn't mind paying for it since the pieces themselves were so cheap. I found a powder-coating business not too far away, chose a color called Squirrel Gray from their paint deck, and quickly became their new favorite customer. On my third visit, the man helping me unload chairs from the back of our truck said, "You must have a very large backyard."

Finding cushions hasn't always been easy. Perhaps one day I'll invest in high-quality custom cushions that fit perfectly, but for now, I find ready-mades that are good enough, though I have learned to prioritize colorfast outdoor fabrics (ordinary fabrics can fade alarmingly in just a few weeks). When it comes to creating beautiful, meaningful places, money can sometimes be more hurdle than help, and thrifty ingenuity always feels good.

MAPLEHURST
Circa
1880
The
Mark Hughes
House

A House with a Name

In books, my favorite houses all have names. Manderley. Howards End. The Herb of Grace. Our Florida home was nameless. It was a lovely little house with exterior walls made of the seashell stucco known as coquina. Except for those pale pink and creamy white seashells, the house was an ordinary builder's home in an ordinary suburban neighborhood. The palm trees and orange trees visible from the windows were extraordinary, or so it seemed to me coming from Chicago, but the interior of the home lacked personality. Soon after moving in, we replaced some outdated light fixtures with large statement pieces. I spray-painted one bright brassy chandelier turquoise. We replaced the old hardware on the white cabinets with knobs carved from turquoise glass and laid an antique runner on the floor. We painted the little front room in a delicate blue-green shade called White Rain. By the time we had finished—and it did not take us long to finish—our little Florida home looked jewel-like and special.

Our seashell house was almost a blank slate. I never considered how previous residents had decorated the place—I simply chose a beachy palette and went for it. But in moving to Pennsylvania, we moved to a house with a name. More accurately, we moved to a house with two names, which meant this house had an established personality and a long history that asked for our respect. The name we use most often is, of course, Maplehurst. That name has been used for the house at least since the turn of the twentieth century and was likely given when the parallel rows of maple trees were first planted from one end of the long driveway to the other. The second name speaks to origins and local history and is "The Mark Hughes House." That name is now on the wooden sign that swings in the breeze where the driveway meets the street. This was the name as we read it on many of the papers we received during the initial real estate transaction, but if I could go back I might ask our sign maker to carve the name as "The Mark and Priscilla Hughes House." Her name might not have been on the land ownership deed, but surely she shaped the place as much as he.

Mark and Priscilla were descendants of William Penn's first Quaker colonists. Like Penn, they were of Welsh origin and were both members of the local Friends Meetinghouse. When they built this redbrick farmhouse on a parcel of land purchased from Mark's father, they had two daughters. A third would be born to them in the house, delivered by the local doctor, whose own son would one day marry that third little Hughes girl. One year in October as I turned the corner near the Society of Friends Meetinghouse that sits high on a rise overlooking our small borough's main street, it occurred to me that Mark and Priscilla might be buried in the graveyard behind the redbrick building. A few weeks later, during a visit from my parents, we drove over and parked near the old covered sheds once used to protect the carriage horses while their owners sat together indoors in prayerful silence. The graveyard lay under a canopy of trees. The stones were quite small and sometimes difficult to read, but we found three markers: one for Mark, one for Priscilla, and one for their eldest daughter. Somehow, seeing those names and imagining those bodies laid to rest almost within reach of the house they had built—the house I now call mine—startled me. I had expected to find them there, yet still I was surprised. The people who had been only names took on flesh, and became as real as my own husband, my own daughter. We already felt ourselves to be simply the home's current caretakers, but in that moment I knew it was true. What I call *mine* is always something given and will always be something I one day give away.

While the tradition of naming houses is not so well established in my own country, I wish it were. Give a name to a place and suddenly that place feels less like an object and more like a subject with its own personality, its own needs, its own separate identity. It might seem whimsical to some to invest a material place with personality. I still remember literature teachers describing the so-called pathetic fallacy, in which a writer invests some nonhuman thing with human traits. *Pathetic. Fallacy.* Whatever those words may mean in context, the label sounds damning. But I think most people who have ever loved a place or a house, or even read a book in which the house became a character in the story, know deep down there is nothing pathetic or tragically sentimental about honoring our places with a separate sense of self. Maplehurst may not be human, but this place has been shaped by human love and human desires, by human dreams and human effort.

Maybe houses are like velveteen rabbits. Maybe they come alive with our love.

When Jonathan and I were facing a difficult decision about redesigning our driveway and wondering whether or not we would replant the rows of maple trees as they aged and fell, a friend who is also a garden designer gave me the most wonderful, bracing advice. Knowing I was struggling with endless design possibilities, Julie cut right through my confusion with these words: "Honor the past. Maplehurst has always had a long, straight driveway. Maybe it always should." With those three words—"honor the past"—a whole slew of possibilities fell right off my list. Then the right choice became clear: the driveway would stay where it was, but I would forgo replanting the two straight rows of trees. Instead, I would let the big trees linger on, while I planted small groves and left certain views open toward the horizon. There is a feeling of spaciousness now as we drive the distance from street to house, but there is also continuity. From the street, you see the house framed by leaves, just as you always have.

We modern people live in a world of almost endless prospects. We have shrugged off so many of the limitations that guided previous generations. This is good in many ways, but it does make some things harder. With so many options, including so many placemaking possibilities, how do we choose? What will guide us? "Honor the past" has become a guide for me in this place. It doesn't neatly answer every question, but it does help rein in the possibilities to a more manageable scope. We have made drastic changes here for modern living, but we have not made every drastic change that we've conceived. In this place, we have received a legacy, and we are cultivating one. We are middlemen. We are caretakers living in between the past of this place and its future.

In this place, we have received a legacy, and we are cultivating one. We are middlemen. We are caretakers living in between the past of this place and its future.

Inspiration

Favorite Books with Great House Characters

The Secret Garden
Frances Hodgson Burnett

To the Lighthouse
Virginia Woolf

Howards End
E.M. Forster

Rebecca
Daphne du Maurier

Pilgrim's Inn
Elizabeth Goudge

Little House in the Big Woods
Laura Ingalls Wilder

I Capture the Castle
Dodie Smith

The Children of Green Knowe
Lucy M. Boston

Winter Solstice
Rosamunde Pilcher

The Big House: A Century in the Life of an American Summer Home
George Howe Colt

A Way Station

The words *community* and *hospitality* sit differently with me now, twelve years after moving here. While we still lived in Florida, while I was dreaming of a new house and a different kind of home that could also somehow lead us to a different way of life, I kept hearing those words in my mind. I thought their meanings were simple and straightforward. I had recently returned to Chicago to visit with a longtime friend who had moved into a big old house during my absence. Staying in a guest room on her third floor, knowing it had once belonged to a servant, I realized the obvious: old houses were built to accommodate servants. Old houses had human-sized rooms rather than so-called great rooms, but they had more bedrooms than a typical new home with the same square footage. Even our small Chicago apartment had a tiny bedroom and bathroom in the back for a maid, though the previous owners had combined the kitchen and bedroom to create a larger eat-in kitchen. Waking in my friend's guest bedroom and feeling the weight of my longing for a new kind of life like a heavy blanket laid over me, I realized that Jonathan and I needed to look for an old house with many bedrooms if we wanted to fulfill our still-fuzzy dream of creating a place we could share.

In Florida, I began to dream not only of an old rambling house with many bedrooms but, in particular, of a *farm*house with land. What I could never puzzle out—until I first laid eyes on Maplehurst—was how a country house could be a hospitable, community-minded place. I understood that day in July, having flown up from Florida to quickly find a house, when we first drove down the long driveway with our real estate agent. Here was a farmhouse, but where Guernsey cattle had once grazed in the fields, there were now new houses. Those houses represented neighbors. I could easily imagine the backyard barbecues. Though it was a hot day, I could already see how kids on bicycles would fill the sidewalks as the summer sun set. My simple understanding of community and hospitality now had a simple solution. These people in these houses would be our community. We would tend this place like a farmer, and good things would grow.

We began that first spring by hosting a neighborhood-wide Easter egg hunt, and we did that for many years. Good things and good relationships did grow, but twelve years have also shown me that life ebbs and flows. Seasons come and go, as do people. Some of the traditions I assumed we would keep forever were pulled from our hands during a pandemic and then—having learned a few lessons ourselves—not picked up again by choice. Good things are not good because they stay the same forever. For a while at first, our third-floor bedroom was lived in by Elsa's babysitter. Later, she moved out of that room and our oldest child moved in. Houses do grow with us, as do the kinds of community we cultivate and the hospitality we offer. I first welcomed strangers. Then I welcomed teenagers. I once lived in a home with small children. I now live in a home with young adults. Where once I could invite anyone over at any time, I now understand that I am not the only adult in this place, and my children need rest and privacy too. These days the hospitality I practice is as likely to be offered to my own family as it is to someone else.

I've learned that the best hospitality is simply showing up as myself living as I always do.

Those words, *community* and *hospitality,* feel different now because I've learned that they are, in actuality, other-oriented. They aren't primarily about me or my needs. When I look back, I realize that though I used these words, what I was really talking about was friendship. I was lonely. I wanted companions. Without thinking it through, deep down I imagined hospitality as a way to win friends. We had experienced that in Chicago during those wild formative years of early marriage and parenthood. I wanted fellow pilgrims and thought I could attract them with my house. But this house has turned out to be more of a way station. Pilgrims come and pilgrims go. Some stay for a night. Some stay for a while. Some I thought would be lifetime friends were called on to other relationships and other places. And friends I thought I had lost have turned up again and again and again. Now I imagine community and hospitality and companionship like three distinct circles in a Venn diagram. They do sometimes overlap, and when they do, it's magic. But often they do not, and that can be pretty magical too.

Pilgrims on their way leave gifts, whether they realize it or not. I think of my friend Amy's father, who had only been here for one brief visit before he casually asked if we'd ever thought of switching our family room and dining room. That suggestion was better than a light-bulb moment. It was more like a sunrise moment. Switching those rooms meant that our too-tight dining room became a cozy den, and our too-open family room became a spacious place that could hold our table with all of its extra leaves installed. Thanks to some other pilgrims who have stopped awhile here, I have learned how to love and how to serve even when I'm tired and running on empty. I've learned how to make better coffee. I've learned how to listen. I've learned that sharing what we have needn't be complicated or fussy. I've learned that the best hospitality is simply showing up as myself living as I always do. With guests, we keep our usual weekly rhythms, but with an open door and these words on our lips: *you are welcome in this place.*

Common Prayer

Inspiration

Guest Room Comforts

Our first guest room at Maplehurst was a bedroom tucked into the eaves of the third floor. Because it was impossible to carry a box spring up the winding back stairs, we drove an hour to IKEA one week after moving day in order to secure a queen-sized bed frame with a slatted base that could be assembled in the room. Our first houseguests arrived a week later. That bed is still there, though the bedroom has belonged to our oldest child for many years now. Our guests now stay in the Black Barn we built four years after coming to Maplehurst.

Here are some of the special touches I like to include in any bedroom I offer a guest:

- A water bottle and glass carafe
- An essential oil diffuser with oils
- A plug-in white noise machine
- A down-alternative mattress topper
- Bamboo or linen sheets
- A bath towel, hand towel, and wash cloth in a color reserved for guests
- A basket or bowl with snacks
- A guest book
- Wi-Fi password
- A box of tissues
- A writing desk
- An electric kettle, mugs, black and herbal teas; milk in a nearby refrigerator if possible
- Coffee (we've had different coffee setups in the Black Barn over the years—we currently offer a small Nespresso machine with recyclable coffee pods like the ones you'll find in every European hotel room)
- At least two pillows with zip-on allergy covers

We Are Never Alone in a Library

So many of the changes we have made in this place have been made with others in mind. Most of the alterations have prioritized hospitality. We built a barn for gathering, but our kitchen is overdue for a renovation and we never have managed to refinish all of our floors. We added more finished space for parking, but the main driveway's asphalt still needs repair. We love to dream of parties, though even as we dream, the plaster in our back stairwell continues to crack and chip and fail. Are we unusually selfless in our placemaking? Or are we merely dreamers captured by thoughts of Big Things while the little things all around us go unnoticed? I am never quite sure, but I do know that only twice have I considered something big primarily for my own enjoyment, and both projects, once finished, cared for me in times of enormous grief. I don't think I'm advocating selfishness. I'm merely pointing out that when we set out to create a spacious place, that place will prove spacious for us too.

My first big, possibly selfish desire for Maplehurst was a flower garden. I've written about that dream in other books, and I've shared as well how the garden in its first truly beautiful, abundant summer became a place of comfort for me, my newly widowed sister, and her children. I had worried a garden devoted only to beauty would be impractical, but it offered respite and healing in the most practical ways. Don't let anyone tell you beauty isn't as real as medicine or money. I find it is much more real, in fact. My second big, possibly selfish desire for Maplehurst was to turn the parlor into a library with a full wall of built-in bookshelves. My husband considered building the shelves himself, but

W B YEATS
MARINER
Poetry Speaks
Norton Anthology of Modern Poetry
The Five Quintets
HARRY POTTER
THE ATLAS OF BEAUTY
SEAMUS HEANEY

we held back because he had so many other more important projects on his list, and because we knew that something so permanent needed to be the highest quality we could manage. Maplehurst deserved nothing less.

The problem with being a visionary is that you see things, whether you want to see them or not. For years, every time I sat in my armchair near the stone fireplace in the front parlor, I would picture the wall across from the hearth covered floor to ceiling with shelves. I didn't want to see this, but I couldn't stop seeing it. During the pandemic, when the barn we had built for guests was being used as a schoolroom for our four children, Jonathan and I decided to take the plunge and call a local cabinetmaker. I had been receiving his brochures in the mail for years. Actually, as I type this, it occurs to me that I have not received a brochure like that since. But finding him was easy, and explaining our vision to him was easy. Only the waiting was difficult, because it coincided with a major crisis in the life of one of our children. We were suffering the kind of pain that is so emotional and spiritual it becomes physical, too, and we were suffering alone because of the isolation of those days. And on one of the darkest days of all, the cabinetmaker called and asked if we were ready for installation.

Were we ready? No, I don't think we were. I was so sad and so afraid in those days that I couldn't think about much else, but without thinking we said yes, and within a few days our parlor had

VINES
THE HISTORY OF CHRISTIANITY
ROGET'S THESAURUS
CHURCHILL
SURRENDER
National Parks
WORLD ATLAS OF NATIONS

I am buoyed up by the knowledge that God gives good gifts to his children even when we feel ourselves undeserving of abundance or extravagant beauty.

become a library. My older son became very excited about the empty shelves and tackled—almost entirely on his own—the job of moving our books into their stunning new green-painted home. The shelves were so beautiful, seeing my books again, like so many friends, was such a gift, and the fact of it happening the very week our pain had brought us to a precipice, well, it seemed to me then—and it seems to me still—that we had not been alone in our decision to build those shelves. Receiving them was like receiving a gift from the God who sees. The God who is with us. The God who goes on giving good gifts even when our hearts are breaking.

I have always resonated with the words William Nicholson wrote in his screenplay for the C.S. Lewis film *Shadowlands*: "We read to know that we are not alone."[7] In my library, I am never alone. I am surrounded by the company of so many books I have loved. And I am buoyed up by the knowledge that God gives good gifts to his children even when we feel ourselves undeserving of abundance or extravagant beauty. My child survived her terrible ordeal, and we survived as well. Our hearts have healed, yet I have never stopped feeling the immense goodness and comfort given to me in that room. It is a small room, one that became even smaller with the addition of those shelves. But it is small in the way that a human heart is small. It is the beating heart of our home. It is the center.

If You Also Long for a Library

I've dreamed of a library complete with a library ladder since I was a child collecting Nancy Drew books. I can still remember my mother's surprise when I asked for books one Christmas when I was around thirteen. The first piece of furniture Jonathan and I bought together before we were married was a bookcase in pale blond wood.

If you are still waiting for the library of your dreams, here are some ideas for the meantime:

- Begin a collection of seasonal picture books; such books are works of art whether or not you have children in the home, and they can be packed away and pulled out with other holiday decorations.
- Dedicate a space for cookbooks in the kitchen. Few things are more cheerful than a row of colorful spines, and cooking from a book is always easier than cooking from a screen.
- Get creative with DIY shelving, even adding shelves over doorways for a cozy cottage look.
- Minimalism may be stylish, but remember that book stacks don't count as clutter.
- This is an old tip from the early days of Pinterest, but wooden spice racks like the sort sold at IKEA make wonderful wall-hung bookshelves. Front-facing books are also more likely to be grabbed by young readers, and wooden racks can easily be painted in fun colors.
- Bedside tables by every bed are a must—not for phones but for books!
- There is a place for thrift, but if you truly love a book, it is worth passing over the tatty paperback and seeking out a beautiful edition.
- One of the best gifts my husband ever gave me was a handheld embosser that marks a page in a book with the words *From the Library of Christie Purifoy*. Much better than a sticker or label.

When the Dream We Did Not Dream Comes True

If you are a dreamer like me, then a primary responsibility of your life will be learning to recognize all the surprising ways in which your dreams have actually come true. Promises are kept and visions are realized all the time, but if we don't slow down and really consider things, we can easily miss seeing the good story woven into our lives. We can forget what it felt like to long for something that seemed out of reach, because always, it seems, there is more to reach for. Gratitude is really an invitation to rest. We pull back our reaching arms and hearts and say, *Yes, this.* Also, dreams generally don't come true gradually and in ways we can clearly perceive. In my experience, it feels like nothing is happening, the thing we hoped for will never come true, it is impossible, until one day we look around and think, *Here it is. My dream. And after all this time.*

Today, as I type these words out, the very first winter snowflakes are whipping through the air. I walked over to my bedroom window to take a picture. I pointed my camera toward the flower garden down below, but then I shifted to get a better image. Bright white snowflakes look nice against the brown of the garden, but they look magnificent against the black walls of Grammy's cottage. Though once it was but a fuzzy idea in our minds, the notion of a multigenerational home was a large part of the dreaming that propelled our family from our seashell-stuccoed house in Florida to this farmhouse

Gratitude is really an invitation to rest.

life in Pennsylvania. Watching the snowflakes beat against the walls of the cottage while golden light shone from its large front window, I caught my breath. This cottage was a dream we'd given up on—not in despair, merely resignation. Yet here we are.

When Jonathan and I first came to Pennsylvania—with our youngest still so very heavy in my belly—we told our real estate agent we wanted to look at houses with guest apartments and mother-in-law suites. We knew we wanted a property for a lifetime of living, and we dimly understood that lifetimes include aging parents and even our own aging selves. We looked at one property with a separate guesthouse. We looked at one old house with beautiful living quarters on the third floor. We looked at one farmhouse with a horse barn and asked ourselves if the barn could be converted. Could grandparents live where horses stood nodding their heads at us? Ultimately, none of those properties made sense. Some were too expensive, some needed too many repairs, and some had too much land, or not enough. We felt like Goldilocks except that even Maplehurst, when we found it, did not seem like a perfect fit. Since then, I've learned that perfect is something we make. Perfect unfolds over time. Perfect even shows up in things we dislike and things we would change. Perfect is a complicated story.

We never knew exactly which parents we were planning for. Neither my parents nor my husband's seemed inclined to move to Pennsylvania. Eventually, we began to discuss it with Jonathan's parents in Texas, but those conversations never really gained ground. I decided we'd been mistaken in that aspect of our vision. Instead, we enjoyed welcoming both sets of parents for stays in the Black Barn, and we continued to plan for a grand family reunion that would include my parents, my siblings, and all of our many nieces and nephews. The idea of that reunion had been an igniting spark for building our guest barn in the first place. Then we faced the pandemic, first with incredulity, then with growing horror, and finally with acceptance and accommodation. That strange season unsettled many of us. We no longer took it for granted that we could hop on a plane and see one another whenever we liked. We no longer believed that our parents would always be just fine on their own. As well, house prices in Texas had climbed sky-high. "Maybe now," Jonathan's father asked, "is the right time to sell?"

Here is what I mean about dreams coming true in unexpected ways: we dreamed of a life

together, but we were given a death to share. Jonathan's mother and father moved quickly once they decided to come, but even those few months witnessed a precipitous and mysterious decline in my father-in-law's health. We imagined how Jonathan and his father would work together here on the property. We cleared space in our shed for his woodworking tools. We pictured the cottage he and his wife would design together. We wondered how it would work for the two of them to adjust to so few square feet. Instead, not long after settling into the Black Barn, when we had just begun the process of hiring an architect and securing building permission, Jonathan's father entered hospice care at home. He died, surrounded by his family, on the day after Thanksgiving, not even three months after moving here.

Sometimes dreams come true like a box of pure joy wrapped in good cheer and happiness. Sometimes dreams come true like a box of grief wrapped in mercy and grace. Because he died in our home, the death of Jonathan's father was not accompanied by travel and trouble and difficult questions. It was accompanied by peace and quiet and the gift of presence. We never worried, *Do we take the children out of school?* We simply let them visit between homework and dinner. We never fretted, *What will Mom do on her own?* All that was required was to be where we were with the people we loved. And isn't that what a home is for?

Sometimes dreams come true like a box of pure joy wrapped in good cheer and happiness. Sometimes dreams come true like a box of grief wrapped in mercy and grace.

Certain gifts become gifts only in hindsight. They are gifts we unwrap as we remember. For years, we have kept two wooden Adirondack chairs at the top of a hill that rises along the eastern side of our long driveway. The wood is softening and growing a bouquet of lichen, but the chairs remain as the sign of the gift we were given. Every time I pass them, usually with a pile of mail in my hands or a dog tugging on a leash, I mentally step out of my current circumstances and remember Jonathan's parents sitting in those chairs to watch the sunset. The days of their togetherness here at Maplehurst were brief, lasting only from the first cool weather front of September until the first serious cold of late November. We could not know how brief that season would be. Only now can we see and give thanks for all that we were given. As a gift, it is small enough to encompass with our hands, but it is weighty. It is as if we were given solid gold.

A Shared Life

There must be infinite ways for generations to make a home together. Here are some of the gifts we have particularly treasured:

- Watching our child's grandmother become grandmother to all the neighborhood children
- Homework help and tutoring with someone who isn't Mom or Dad
- Weekly texts that say, "I'm headed to the grocery store. Can I pick up anything for you?"
- Annual texts that say, "Did you see it's snowing outside?"
- Sharing meals, sharing birthdays, sharing holidays, sharing casual chats while watering the garden pots and delivering the mail
- Less fear of the future
- More joy in the present

Community Pool

Words can surprise us with their hidden depths. Step into a word expecting a puddle on solid ground, anticipating a little splash around your ankles, and you might just find you have fallen in over your head. You might find that you are swimming in unfamiliar waters and loving it. The word *community* has been like that for me at Maplehurst. When we first desired this place and searched for it, we were motivated by loneliness. We had lost the first real community of our married life when we moved away from Chicago, and Florida taught us that such things are not easily replaced. We raced here as if on a river called hope, and the neighborhood of newly built houses all around the "hurst"—or hill—where our new house sat felt like the answer to all the questions we'd been asking. Here was our house. Here was our home. Here was our new community.

Seven months after moving in, we still had yet to meet a single neighbor. It seemed to me that the evergreens planted along our property boundary effectively screened us from distant views and from our neighbors. Also, I was well tethered to the house by a newborn's frequent naps. During those months, it dawned on me that our Pennsylvania neighborhood had none of the community features we had appreciated in Florida. There was no community pool and not even a community playset. Where did mothers of young children gather? I tried the local library, I tried taking my baby in her stroller for walks, but new friends remained elusive. Hosting our first neighborhood-wide Easter egg hunt that first spring introduced us to dozens of neighbors all at once. The tide of loneliness began to shift, though I had yet to feel as if that word *community* had much purchase on my actual life.

Maplehurst is a place fueled by my daydreams. Or, as my friend Summer once said with such prescience it brought me to tears, Maplehurst is my inner life made visible. I do sometimes feel as if my mind is a balloon. The very second my body is engaged in some repetitive action (washing dishes, washing my hair), my thoughts float away as if on a breeze. In these reveries, I have seen flower gardens growing, parties unfolding, and trees planted in some new spot. I have seen French doors where there were only windows, bookshelves where there was a bare wall, and I have dreamed of a walkway illuminated by candle-lit luminaria at dusk. I dream and then return to my waking life with some new desire or idea or vision.

Strangely, there are never other people in my daydreams. Yet one of the gifts of this place has been all the ways it is too much for us alone. Even if we had all of the requisite skills and knowledge, there are not enough minutes in the day to tick every box and complete every necessary task. Even as I write these words, some part of my mind is wondering who I can call to take a look at our radiators and whether the plaster on our younger daughter's ceiling is about to fail. The long crack has been there for quite some time, but the ominous bulge seems new. I may not dream of other people, but I have learned how necessary they are. Necessary for repair and for healing this house. Necessary as recipients for the beauty I do love to cultivate. A candle I will light for myself, but something as ambitious as a path lined with paper-bag lanterns for a holiday party is always for someone else. Even the candy-filled eggs I had imagined hidden down the long green stretches of our property asked for a crowd of children to search them out.

Maplehurst is the work of many hands—hands that extend deep into the past and wide across this present moment. There are the unknown hands that laid the first line of locally made bricks. There are the hands that carved Roman numerals in the frames of each window to indicate its position in the house. There are the hands that did the unseen work of years: tending fires, washing windows, and sweeping the wide front porch. Then there are the hands I have known. John and Kelly restored every window. Bill repaired the bricks and mortar, the old copper-lined Yankee gutters, and so much more. Amish men built the barn, and a friend of a friend (who then became our friend) finished its interior. When I remember what community actually looked like for the first few years of living here, it is a community of helpers that I see. They spent so much time here that they became to us as familiar as family. Some of them became the people we still call when we have some need that goes beyond bricks and plaster.

The voices of this community also ring in my mind. We had come to Maplehurst with desire and with vision, but rarely will we dream the size of dream others will dream for us. Quite a few of our helpers asked me over the years where we planned

to put the pool, until I eventually grew frustrated. Complaining to Jonathan, I said, "Do they think we're made of money? Of course we can't put in a pool when so much needs repair." For eight years, we insisted there would never be a pool at Maplehurst, but then the pandemic temporarily offered Jonathan a little more income and our family a lot more time at home. Only then did a desire inside of me that I had never allowed myself to acknowledge begin to rise like a swimmer returning from a deep dive. Our longed-for family reunion had been planned for the summer of 2020, but with that dream on hold, we began to consider how good it really would be to have a backyard pool for our eventual summertime gathering. I could hear our landscaper friend Pete pointing out just the spot, and I could hear Amy's father saying that an old farmhouse deserved its own elegant version of a swimming hole. I began to let myself remember how much I had loved swimming during the first eighteen years of my life. As a competitive swimmer, lifeguard, and swim coach, I had practically lived in sunshine and chlorine until I married and moved away from Texas. Truthfully, though I had stopped swimming years before, I had never stopped dreaming about pools. In my dreams, I was often in the water again.

Of course, writing it all out in a few paragraphs is swift and sure compared with our actual living. By the time our name rose to the top of the pool builder's waiting list, the price had risen considerably and that extra income had tapered off. We were left, as we have so often been left, to take a leap of faith, to discern not what felt safest but what was right and best, and to consider the needs of all those others we hoped would gather here. As well, we were led by the many voices that had spoken of a pool at a time when we could not see past the next major repair. A community had told us Maplehurst deserved a pool, and while we could easily forgo such a thing for ourselves, we have learned to listen to others. That is one way we try to live as caretakers rather than owners. We have learned not to stand in the way of good things for this home.

Eventually, we said yes, and the diggers moved in. By late August, we had a neat rectangular hole behind the house where the old driveway had once tied its loop around the property. All winter, the pool seemed still unreal, despite its depths clearly visible from the kitchen windows. In late spring, the pool was finally filled with water. When I first jumped in, the water was cold, and in an instant I was a teenager again, leaping into the water for a winter swim practice. With my whole self I remembered how it was when I was young, when I felt as if I could swim forever without any need to stop. I realized over the course of that first summer, as I swam up and down and up and down each morning, that something precious had been given back to me though I had not gone in search of it. Once more, I was home. Home again.

Welcome Home Again

Here at the end, I want at last to tell you that the title of this book is all wrong. It isn't really possible to create places that will care for us. It only seems at first and for a little while that this is what we are doing. Eventually, however, the truth emerges: everything in life is given and our job is simply to receive. Yet even our receiving can be a creative act. *Praise God from whom all blessings flow.*

Our culture has recently become obsessed with manifestation. The idea seems to be that if we figure out what we really want, we have the power within ourselves to will those things into reality. There is a kind of logic in the idea, and I have little doubt that it has worked—or seemed to work—for some people. My objection isn't one of efficacy (*does it work?*). Rather, my objection is this: *I don't want to play God.* When I speak of dreams and visions—like my dream of a farmhouse home—I am not really talking about something I decided to want. I am speaking of something much more mysterious and much more relational. I am talking about revelation. I am speaking about a life of faith.

Our own plans and shallow desires can take us quite far in life. And there is nothing at all wrong with this. It's how we begin, putting one foot in front of the other and learning about ourselves in the process. My own plans carried me all the way through a graduate degree and three children until we landed in Florida, and I finally began to ask, *Is this it? What now?* Perhaps real beginnings often come in the middle of life. I suspect more and more that this is the way of it. My true beginning started at the point that I ran out of the logical next-step options given to me by my family of origin, culture, and temperament: college graduation, marriage, graduate school, children, first job, first house, a few moves. I had some achievements, I even had a few opportunities, and I was grateful. I wasn't struggling with a sense of discontent. What I found myself lacking was vision. I wanted some hold on the bigger picture, and I felt sure that whatever this bigger picture was it didn't revolve around me and the things I wanted on any given day. It wasn't only that I didn't know what to do or where to go—it was that I lacked any sense of the why. *What is the story of the world? What is the story of my life? How do these stories intersect?*

Of course, I can only state my questions so plainly because I am writing in retrospect. Nothing was so clear at the time. I knew that I was unhappy, but I was also aware that my unhappiness felt more like a holy discontent rather than a simple lack of gratitude. In some sense, my Christian upbringing—though it had carried me thus far—began to fail me at this moment. I had been taught, rightly, to value God's will over my own. I had been taught to pray, *Thy will be done*. In those days, I wished that God would tell me what to do and where to go so I could simply obey. But I believe our maker desires more than obedience. Our maker desires to grow wisdom in us. When we are wise, we can see what God sees, and we can

So let us make our places. Let us tend our homes. It will cost us everything. It will give us everything in return.

discern how to move in that direction. With wisdom, we can partner with God. We can participate in his dreams for us and for this world he so loves.

With wisdom, we lean into the fullness of the prayer that Christ gave to us: *thy kingdom come, thy will be done, on earth as it is in heaven.*[8] Heaven on earth is what God wants, and isn't that what we want too? Was this dream of a house to call home, a place where we could welcome others, my desire or God's? I think the only possible answer is yes. Is this home for me or for others? Again, the answer is yes. Will making and tending this place require self-sacrifice or will it offer self-care? Yes. The wisdom of heaven turns everything inside out and upside down. We will leave our homes to find them. We will wander and come home. We will choose a simple and free way of life, but the price we pay for it will be all that we are. When we say yes and walk through this narrow door, we will find ourselves in a spacious place.

So let us make our places. Let us tend our homes. It will cost us everything. It will give us everything in return. And over time, all mountains shall be lowered, all valleys raised up, and we will know the truth of those words spoken by poets and mystics: there is a home prepared for each of us, and in that place, all shall finally be well.

ACKNOWLEDGMENTS

Thank you to the great team at Harvest House—especially to Heather Green for being such a creative, thoughtful partner in the making of beautiful books. Also, thank you to Ruth Samsel for encouraging me to revisit my love for placemaking.

Thank you to John Blase for consistently solid advice given generously and at just the right moments. I am also grateful to my friend Ned Bustard for first suggesting I write about my love for dollhouses. Thank you for giving me your enthusiastic permission to incorporate material I wrote for your book *Ordinary Saints: Living Everyday Life to the Glory of God* in the opening essay of this book.

My house has become a home in large part because of those friends and family who have joined me here. Thank you, Nathan and Melissa Baird, Lisa-Jo Baker, Amy Knorr, and Myrna Purifoy, especially. And many thanks to my creative, talented sister Kelli Campbell-Goodnow who always insisted I could learn to take photographs, too. Your portraits and snapshots of my house and family have become my most precious heirlooms. Lastly, thank you to my husband, Jonathan. I dream it, you build it, and together, we make a very good team. I love you, and I love the life we have made and received together.

TIMBER
PRESS

NOTES

Part 1 Epigraph: Mary Norton, *The Borrowers* (Harcourt, 2003), 49.

The essay titled "(Doll)House Repairs" was originally published in a slightly different form as "Home Repairs: Better and More Beautiful" in *Ordinary Saints: Living Everyday Life to the Glory of God* (Square Halo Books, 2023), 11–14. Reprinted by permission of the editor and publisher.

[1] Myquillyn Smith, *Welcome Home: A Cozy Minimalist Guide to Decorating and Hosting All Year Round* (Zondervan, 2020), 40.

Part 2 Epigraph: Kenneth Grahame, *The Wind in the Willows* (Atheneum Books for Young Readers, 1983), 96.

[2] W.H. Auden, *For the Time Being: A Christmas Oratorio* (Princeton University Press, 2013).

[3] Wendell Berry, "How to Be a Poet," *Poetry*, January 2001, https://www.poetryfoundation.org/poetrymagazine/issue/71366/january-2001.

[4] Elizabeth Goudge, *Pilgrim's Inn* (Coward-McCann, 1948), 59.

[5] Jen Pollock Michel, *In Good Time: 8 Habits For Reimagining Productivity, Resisting Hurry, and Practicing Peace* (Baker Books, 2022), 50.

[6] T.S. Eliot, "Burnt Norton," *The Four Quartets* (Harcourt, Inc., 1943), 177.

Part 3 Epigraph: Elizabeth von Arnim, *The Enchanted April* (Virago Press, 2011), 57.

[7] William Nicholson, *Shadowlands* (Price Entertainment, Spelling Films International, 1993).

[8] Matthew 6:10 reads, "Thy kingdom come, / Thy will be done, / On earth as it is in heaven."

ABOUT THE AUTHOR

Christie Purifoy is a writer and gardener who loves to create welcoming places where plants and people can thrive. She is the author of many books, including, most recently, *Seedtime and Harvest: How Gardens Grow Roots, Connection, Wholeness, and Hope.*

Christie earned a PhD in English Literature from the University of Chicago before trading the classroom for an old Pennsylvania farmhouse called Maplehurst. Along with her husband and children, she frequently welcomes guests to the Maplehurst Black Barn.

CHRISTIEPURIFOY.COM

LIFE LESSONS FROM THE FLOWER GARDEN

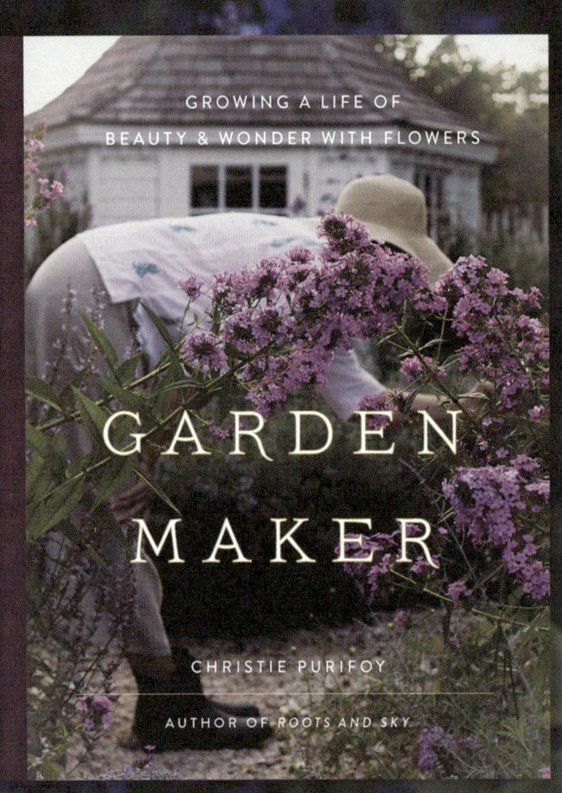

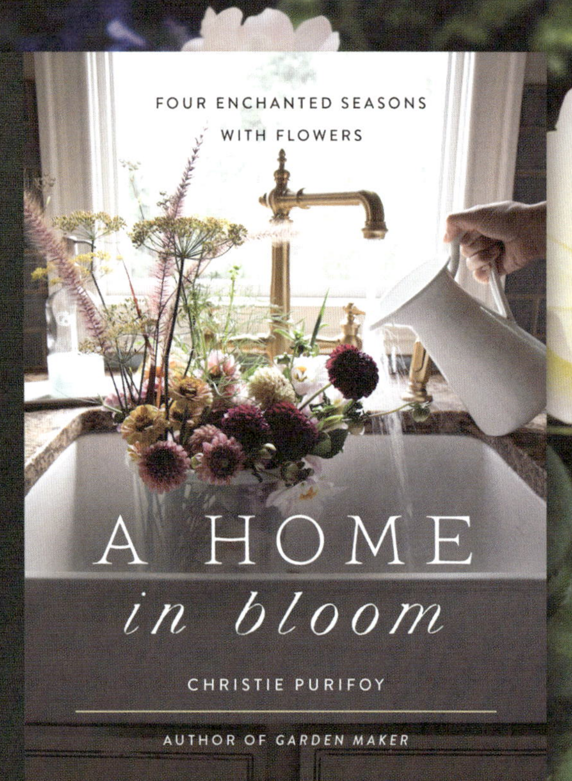

All Scripture verses are taken from the Revised Standard Version of the Bible, Copyright © 1946, 1952, and 1971 the Division of Christian Education of the National Council of the Churches of Christ in the United States of America. Used with permission. All rights reserved.

Published in association with The Bindery Agency, www.TheBinderyAgency.com

Cover design by Faceout Studio, Molly von Borstel
Interior design by Faceout Studio, Paul Nielsen
Photograph on pages 2 and 3 by Kayleigh Reindl.
Photographs on pages 134 (top left, top right, bottom left), 135 (top left), 136 (top left, bottom), 137 (top left), 138 (top left, bottom right), 139, 205 by Alyssa Ruth Photography
All other photography by Christie Purifoy
Cover frame image © Studio Cantath / Shutterstock

This logo is a federally registered trademark of the Hawkins Children's LLC.
Harvest House Publishers, Inc., is the exclusive licensee of this trademark.

A HOUSE TO CALL HOME

Published by Harvest House Publishers
Eugene, Oregon 97408
www.harvesthousepublishers.com

ISBN 978-0-7369-9127-8 (hardcover)
ISBN 978-0-7369-9128-5 (ebook)

Library of Congress Control Number: 2025941464

Printed in China

25 26 27 28 29 30 31 32 33 / RDS / 10 9 8 7 6 5 4 3 2 1